W9-BPS-940

75TH SEASON

National Symphony Orchestra

Leonard Slatkin, Music Director

THE NATIONAL
SYMPHONY
ORCHESTRA

COOKBOOK

www.nationalsymphony.org

Acknowledgments

Chairman	Patty Perkins Andringa
Publishing Editor	Anna G. Pfeiffer
Food Editor	Susan Porter

Special thanks to Katherine Andringa, Debra Bates-Schrott, Bonnie Curry Brose, Nancy Crum, Mark Evans, Ann Friedman, Lonie Landfield, Jennifer Leed, Virginia C. Mars, Barbara A. Moore, Patricia O'Kelly, Deborah Pine, Elizabeth Rowe, Rita Shapiro, Neil Schwartz, Norma Stewart, Alice Weinreb, and Christopher Wolf.

ISBN 0-9771183-0-4

Library of Congress Control Number: 2005930252

Designer and Illustrator: Seth H. Sirbaugh, Bates Creative Group
Printing: Mount Vernon Printing Company

NATIONAL SYMPHONY ORCHESTRA

Initially formed by local musicians, "The National Symphony Orchestra of Washington, D.C." performed three trial concerts in 1930. Conductor Hans Kindler became Music Director and established the NSO as Washington's resident symphony one year later, launching its first season on November 2, 1931 at Constitution Hall. Throughout its history, the NSO has been committed to artistic excellence and the development of America's artistic resources.

By 1935, the Orchestra had found an outdoor summer venue upon the Watergate concert shell on the Potomac River. For 30 years, these "Sunset Symphonies" delighted thousands, whether coupled

as its new home with a gala opening concert on September 9, 1971 under then Music Director Antal Doráti. Featuring Beethoven's Overture "The Consecration of the House" and Stravinsky's *The Rite of Spring,* the program fittingly emphasized youth and sacred beginnings.

In 1980, the NSO traveled to Asia for the first time, with performances in Japan and Korea. The musicians' first USSR tour in 1990 marked Music Director Mstislav Rostropovich's return to his homeland after 16 years in exile. At decade's end in 1999, current Music Director Leonard Slatkin led the Orchestra on its first tour to China.

In 1992, the Orchestra launched its American

Celebrating a Legacy of Excellence

in canoes or picnicking near the Lincoln Memorial. "Summer in the Parks" concerts followed at the Ellipse and Carter Barron Amphitheatre. In 1971, the Orchestra visited Virginia's great outdoors for Wolf Trap's first season. Eight years later, the NSO began its free Memorial Day, Fourth of July, and Labor Day concerts on the West Lawn of the U.S. Capitol.

Touring has been essential to the National Symphony Orchestra's mission since it first traveled beyond Washington along the East Coast and Canada in 1935. The Orchestra first performed at Carnegie Hall on February 2, 1941; that December, the musicians were in Massachusetts when Pearl Harbor was attacked. For the remainder of the tour, they opened every concert with *The Star Spangled Banner.*

The NSO launched its first major international tour in 1959 under Music Director Howard Mitchell with three months of concerts across Central and South America. In 1967, the Orchestra embarked upon its first European tour with stops in Berlin, Vienna, Rome, London, and Madrid. Both of these tours showcased numerous American works.

After 40 years at Constitution Hall, the NSO christened the Kennedy Center Concert Hall

Residencies program. Since then, the NSO has taken up residence in more than a dozen states from Alaska to North Carolina for educational activities and performances.

The NSO has cultivated one of the nation's most expansive series of music education, outreach, and training programs, reaching hundreds of thousands of people each year. From its first season, the Orchestra has offered concerts for young listeners. The 1950s brought Tiny Tots Concerts and NSO Young People's Concerts, still performed for elementary students today. Audiences have enjoyed Family Concerts for more than 30 years and Kinderkonzerts and Ensembles since the 1990s, all usually framed by an instrument "Petting Zoo" and Kids' Chat.

Throughout its history, the NSO has been called upon in times of national celebration and remembrance. From Inauguration concerts for Presidents Roosevelt, Kennedy, and Johnson... to a World War II Victory Concert on the Mall that drew more than 15,000 people... to a 25th anniversary salute to the Peace Corps... to taking part in a post-September 11 "Concert for America," the NSO remains a unique ambassador for the American experience.

CONTENTS

CONTENTS

Danish Buttermilk Bread
Danish Rye Bread
Granola Bread
Easy Oatmeal Bread
Alice's Fluffy Biscuits
Bran Muffins
Coffee Cake
Ruth Tozar's Favorite Coffee Cake
Katie's Coffee Cake
Lemon Bread
Challah
Cornell Bread

SEAFOOD

Tuna and Spinach "Sausage"
Grilled Tuna
Bistro Français Tuna
Paupiette of Lemon Sole with Crabmeat and Coriander Sauce
Dilled Monkfish
Baked Stuffed Red Snapper
Grenadin de Saumon Roti
Yellowtail Snapper or Rockfish Meunière
Pecan Encrusted Salmon
Oven-Baked Smelts
Lotte en Papillot
Soufflé de Poisson à la Florentine with Sauce Mousseline
Psari-Plaki Baked Fish
Monkfish in a Crust of Garlic and Baby Carrots
Lacquered Braised Sea Bass with Ragout of Chanterelles
Shrimp Remoulade
Golden Caviar with Belon Oysters Wrapped in Spinach Leaves
La Salade de Poisson Marine (Marinated Fish Salad)
Baked Mussels
Fisherman's Wharf Cioppino
Oysters Rockefeller
Seafood Strudel
Gingered Shrimp
Carolina Shrimp and Grits
Saucisson de Crustaces
Mussels with Saffron
Shrimp Madeleine
Coquilles St. Jacques Baumanière

Arroz Con Pollo (Chicken with Rice)
Baja California Chicken
Chicken with Lamb and Rice
Chicken Moghlai
Chicken Parmigiana
Chicken Piquant
Germaine's Lemon Chicken
Louise's Chicken Alouette
Poulet au Vinaigre
Puffed Chicken Pockets

CONTENTS

Veal Basket Royal
Osso Buco (Braised Veal Shanks)
Marinated Sweetbreads

PASTA AND RICE
Agnolotti alla Crema
Irena's Lasagne with Bolognese Sauce
Asparagus and Prosciutto Lasagne
Linguini Rosa
Spaghetti Puttanesca alla Moffo
Manicotti
Baked Ziti
Fettuccine Alfredo
Fettuccine Fredde alla Pronto
Tomato Angel Hair Pasta with Basil and Crab
Scapinash con Burro Nocciola, Salvia e Parmigiano
Spaghetti Pie
Trioletta (Pineapple, Cheese, Noodle Squares)
July 4th Pasta Salad
Carol Mason's Pasta Salad
Summer Pasta
Beautiful Baked Rice
Lobster Risotto
Risotto alla Milanese
Shahjanhani Biryani (Spiced Saffron Rice)
Couscous with Onions and Raisins

VEGETABLES
David's Roasted Vegetables
Stuffed Summer Squash
Creamed Leeks
Stuffed Eggplant Casserole
Stuffed Aubergines
Broccoli Soufflé
Carrot Soufflé
Favorite Brussels Sprouts
Smothered Cabbage
Vegetable Mousse
Spinach Casserole
Corn Spoonbread
Corn Soufflé
Sweet Potato Casserole
Sweet Potato Soufflé
Potatoes Supreme
Twice Baked Potatoes Cottage Style
Rosemary Potatoes
Manon's Shoelaces
Spinach Secret Surprise
Stuffed Zucchini Pike Place Market
Turnips Bordelaise
Christmas Tomatoes
Tomato Casserole
Stuffed Mushrooms

Contents

Auntie I's Mandelbrot
Meringue Mushrooms
Armenian Butter Cookies
Val's Brownies
Orange Cookies
Jimmy Carter's Peanut Brittle
Chocolate Peanut Butter Cups
Hillary Rodham Clinton's Original Chocolate Chip Cookies
Chocolate Chip Cookies
Mint Squares
Espresso Brownie
Forgotten Cookies
Kahlua Espresso Coffee Truffles
Syllabub

PASTRIES, PIES AND FRUIT DESSERTS
Baklava à la Grecque
Pashka (Traditional Easter Dessert of Old Russia)
Pineapple Millefeuille
Grapefruit Tart with Chocolate Pecan Crust
Palacsinta (Apricot Pancakes)
Apple Crisp
Crepia aux Pommes
Blueberry Küchen
Bess Truman's Frozen Lemon Pie
Strawberry-Rhubarb Pie
Italian Cheese Pie
Grandmother's Lemon Pie
Hazelnut Fruit Tart
Plum Tart with Almond Cream Base
Plum Tart
Apfelküchen (Apple Tart)
Pêches au Vin de Bordeaux
Saffron Broiled Pineapple
Chocolate Cherry Clafoutis
Strawberries with Balsamic Vinegar

PUDDINGS, MOUSSES AND SOUFFLÉS
Chestnut Mousse
Crema Española (Spanish Cream Egg Custard)
Angela Pia
Crème Brûlée
Mousseline au Chocolat
White Chocolate Mousse
Easy Lemon Mousse
Maple Syrup Mousse
Mousse de Pruneau à l'Armagnac
Soufflé – Orange and Chocolate
Prepare-Ahead Chocolate Soufflé
Orange Marmalade Soufflé
Cold Lemon Soufflé

A tradition of National Symphony Orchestra concerts at the U.S. Capitol began in 1979. Photo from NSO Archives.

Note: *recipes marked with this icon are from the original National Symphony Orchestra Cookbook, published by FANS (Friends Assisting the National Symphony) in 1983.*

APPETIZERS

COLD APPETIZERS

Salmon Caviar Hors d'Oeuvre Roll

SERVES 15

4 tablespoons unsalted butter, extra for jelly roll pan

½ cup flour, preferably unbleached

Salt

2 cups milk, warm

4 eggs, separated, whites stifly beaten

1 teaspoon sugar

6 ounces cream cheese

3 tablespoons sour cream

8 ounces salmon caviar

Butter a 10x15-inch jelly-roll pan well. Do not use wax paper as a lining. In a saucepan, melt 4 tablespoons butter. Add ½ cup flour and a pinch of salt. Stir over medium heat for 1 minute. Preheat oven to 325 degrees.

Gradually add 2 cups warm milk and cook the sauce, stirring constantly for about 4 minutes. Remove saucepan from the heat and blend in 4 egg yolks and 1 teaspoon sugar. Fold in egg whites.

Spread the batter evenly in the prepared pan and bake the roll in a moderately low oven (325 degrees) for 35 to 40 minutes, or until golden brown. With a wooden spoon, blend 6 ounces cream cheese with 3 tablespoons sour cream. Fold in 6 ounces red caviar. Gently fold in 2 ounces more.

Spread the roll with the filling and roll it up. This roll freezes well. It can be kept refrigerated for two days. Serve cold with lightly salted sour cream or reheat gently and serve warm.

Susan Porter
NSO Board Member

Salmon Mousse with Dill Sauce

Serves 4 to 6

2 envelopes unflavored gelatin

⅓ cup water

2 tablespoons lemon juice

1 cup boiling water

2 7½-ounce cans pink salmon (drained, boned, and skinned)

½ cup half and half

½ cup mayonnaise

1 small onion, quartered

DILL SAUCE

1 cup sour cream

1 cup mayonnaise

2 tablespoons lemon juice

2 tablespoons chopped fresh dill

1 tablespoon chopped capers

In container of electric blender, sprinkle gelatin over water and lemon juice and let stand for 5 minutes. Add boiling water and whirl about 30 seconds, until smooth. Add salmon, mayonnaise, half and half and onion; whirl again until smooth.

Pour into an oiled mold, cover with plastic wrap and chill until set (about 3 hours or overnight).

Combine ingredients for dill sauce and chill. Serve with mousse. For a variation of the mousse, dill may be added directly to the mousse and omitted from sauce. The same is true of the capers.

Robert and Marion Merrill
Baritone, Guest Artist

Caviar Mousse

Serves 20

The colors are beautiful. It is especially appropriate for Christmas.

6 ounces red caviar

¼ cup chopped parsley

1 tablespoon grated onion

1 teaspoon grated lemon rind

1 pint sour cream

1 cup heavy cream

1 envelope gelatin

¼ cup water

Freshly ground pepper

In a large bowl combine caviar, parsley, onion and lemon peel. Stir sour cream into this mixture. In a separate bowl whip heavy cream. Sprinkle gelatin over water in a saucepan over low heat until gelatin is dissolved (1 to 2 minutes). Stir gelatin into caviar mixture. Fold into whipped cream and add pepper to taste. Pour mixture into a buttered 4-cup mold. Chill several hours. Unmold onto lettuce. Serve with melba rounds or pumpernickel bread.

Rita Meyer

Ike's Chopped Herring

SERVES 8 AS HORS D'OEUVRE

SERVES 4 AS FIRST COURSE

12-ounce jar herring pieces
with onion
(in wine sauce)

2 slices Jewish rye or
pumpernickel bread

½ large onion

1 large stalk celery

½ medium carrot, scraped

½ green pepper

1 medium apple, peeled
and cored

2 hard-boiled eggs

Sugar and freshly ground
pepper to taste

Drain herring, reserving juice and onions. Soak bread in herring juice. In a food processor with steel blade in place, chop onions from herring jar, ½ onion, celery, carrot, green pepper and apple, only until coarsely chopped.

Add bread, herring, eggs and continue processing until finely chopped. If too dry, add some herring juice; if too wet, add some crackers. Season with sugar and pepper to taste. Do not add salt.

Chill well and serve with crackers as an hors d'oeuvre or on lettuce, garnished with cherry tomatoes, black or green olives as a first course.

Ike Friedlander
Former NSO FANS Member

Cannellini with Shrimp

SERVES 6

1 pound cannellini beans

1 pound shrimp, cleaned and boiled

2 tomatoes, seeded and quartered

Spring onions

Fresh basil

Olive oil and/or roasted garlic oil

Lemon

Salt and pepper to taste

Wash beans in cold water. Put into a large bowl, cover with cold water (½ gallon water for 1 pound beans). Let sit on your countertop overnight. Do not cover.

In the morning put drained beans into a large saucepan, cover with cold water, bring to a boil and then turn the heat down and let them simmer for 20 minutes.

Lift beans out carefully so as not to break them. Cool on a flat plate. Slice shrimp, spring onions, tomatoes and basil. Combine all ingredients in a bowl. Add salt, pepper, olive oil and lemon. Mix and refrigerate. Serve at room temperature; if it is too cold the flavor is dull.

Susan Porter
NSO Board Member

Oeufs en Gelée

SERVES 6

6 eggs

3 packages gelatin

3 cups chicken broth

¼ cup tarragon vinegar

¼ cup water

Chives

Parsley

Salt

Freshly ground pepper

Poach 6 eggs. Chill in refrigerator. Soak 3 packages of gelatin in ¼ cup cold water plus ¼ cup tarragon vinegar. Mix into gelatin 3 cups boiling chicken broth, canned or homemade, until gelatin is dissolved. Add salt and pepper to taste.

Fill baking dish (casserole, Pyrex, etc.) with half of broth mixture and sprinkle with chopped chives and chill. When moderately firm (1 hour or so), arrange eggs on top of jellied broth and pour remaining cool broth on top. Sprinkle chopped parsley on top and chill until firm.

Serve with any dressing, such as Russian, caper, hollandaise or sour cream and caviar.

Mrs. Marvin Braverman
Former NSO Board Member

Pork, Ham and Pistachio Pâté

SERVES APPROXIMATELY 10

"If you can make a meatloaf, then you can make a pâté!"

6 slices bacon

¼ pound pistachios, shelled

1 pound pork sausage

2 teaspoons thyme

2 teaspoons salt

1 teaspoon freshly ground pepper

4 slices ham

¾ pound ground lean pork

2 laurel or bay leaves

Line a terrine or 9x5-inch loaf pan with bacon. Blanch pistachios by pouring boiling, salted water over them, allowing them to sit in water briefly. Remove skins.

Start at bottom of pan and put in half the pork sausage, pressing down. Sprinkle half pistachios over sausage and ⅓ of thyme, salt and pepper. Next add a slice of ham, then all ground, lean pork. Sprinkle with more thyme, salt and pepper. Add another layer of ham and rest of pistachios; finish with a layer of sausage. Sprinkle remaining thyme, salt and pepper on top. Decorate with 2 laurel or bay leaves and cover pâté with strips of bacon.

Place terrine in hot water bath in large rectangular pan and bake, covered, in a 400 degree oven for 1 to 1½ hours. Remove from oven and take off lid or aluminum foil. Weight down with a heavy plate and can of tuna so that pâté will settle into fat in terrine. Allow to cool. Place in refrigerator for 24 to 48 hours before serving.

William J. Wooby
Former NSO FANS Member

Chicken Liver Pâté in Aspic

SERVES 12

ASPIC

2 teaspoons unflavored gelatin

1 cup sherry

2 tablespoons sugar

4 tablespoons water

½ teaspoon dried tarragon, crumbled

PÂTÉ

1 pound chicken livers

1 cup milk

¼ cup cognac

1¼ cups (2½ sticks) butter at room temperature

2 cups sliced onion

¼ cup bourbon

¼ cup whipping cream

1¼ teaspoons salt

1 teaspoon fresh lemon juice

Butter an 8x4-inch loaf pan generously and set aside. Dissolve gelatin in a small bowl with ¼ cup sherry. Combine sugar and water in a saucepan over medium-high heat and stir until sugar is dissolved. Continue cooking until mixture is a dark, caramel color (about 8 to 10 minutes). Whisk in remaining ¾ cup sherry and tarragon.

Reduce heat under saucepan and simmer for about 2 minutes. Add gelatin, stirring until dissolved.

Strain through a sieve or damp cheesecloth to remove tarragon crumbs into prepared loaf pan, covering bottom ⅛ inch to ¼ inch. Chill pan to set aspic.

Combine livers, milk, and cognac in a bowl and let soak for 1 hour.

Melt ½ cup of butter in a large skillet over medium heat. Add sliced onions and sauté until browned. Using a slotted spoon, transfer onion mixture to a food processor (fitted with a steel blade) or blender.

Drain livers, discarding liquid. Return skillet to medium-high heat. Sauté livers until they are just pink (about 10 to 12 minutes). Add to onion mixture in a food processor or blender.

Reduce heat under skillet to medium; add bourbon and cook, scraping up any browned bits. Add bourbon and ¼ cup cream to liver mixture; purée until smooth. Let stand until it has cooled to lukewarm.

continued...

Beat remaining ¾ cup butter in a medium bowl until creamy. With food processor or blender running, add butter gradually to liver mixture, blending well. Add salt and lemon juice. Pour into pan over aspic, smoothing on top. Chill in refrigerator.

To serve, run a sharp knife around the inside of pan, dip pan briefly into hot water, and invert pâté onto a serving platter. Garnish with parsley and serve with thinly sliced French bread or an assortment of crackers.

William J. Wooby
Former NSO FANS Member

White Bean and Herb Dip

MAKES 2½ CUPS

2 cloves garlic, peeled

2 15-ounce cans cannellini beans, drained and rinsed

4 tablespoons fresh squeezed lemon juice

3 tablespoons olive oil

1½ teaspoons ground cumin

Salt and pepper to taste

2 tablespoons chopped fresh mint

2 tablespoons chopped fresh dill

2 teaspoons grated lemon peel

With food processor running, drop garlic cloves in to chop finely; add beans and blend. Stop processor and add lemon juice, olive oil and cumin. Process until smooth and well-blended. Season to taste with salt and pepper. If possible, let mixture rest in refrigerator overnight for flavors to meld.

Mix chopped herbs and lemon zest in a small bowl. Sprinkle over dip and serve with crackers or pita squares. Best served in a flat bowl so herbs can be spread out nicely. Can also mix herbs into dip if planning to eat over several days.

Elizabeth Rowe
Former NSO Assistant Principal Flute

Laura Bush's Guacamole

SERVES 12

8 ripe avocados

4 lemons, juiced

7 shallots, finely chopped

1 jalapeño pepper, seeded and finely chopped

½ bunch cilantro, finely chopped

1 teaspoon black pepper

1 tablespoon salt

Halve and pit avocados and scoop out flesh into a bowl. Mash to desired consistency and mix in remaining ingredients. Cover with plastic wrap and refrigerate for about an hour before serving. Serve with tortilla chips.

First Lady Laura Bush

Chunky Guacamole

SERVES 8 TO 12

4 avocados, preferably Hess

3 tablespoons yellow onion, finely chopped

2 cloves garlic, pressed

2 tablespoon fresh squeezed lime juice

Salt to taste

Peel avocados. Open one, scoop out the shell and mash completely. Add onion, garlic and salt.

Slice and cube remaining three avocados. Slightly mash and mix to a consistency you prefer. Add lime juice and mix. Taste for salt. Serve with chips.

Emily Porter Gerson

Seafood Spread

SERVES 8 TO 10

¾ pound crabmeat or shrimp, cooked and chopped

1 8-ounce package cream cheese

¾ cup mayonnaise

1 cup shredded Swiss, Gruyère or cheddar cheese

2 tablespoons capers

1 tablespoon lemon juice

1 tablespoon dill

Salt and pepper to taste

Worcestershire sauce

2 tablespoons dried onions, minced

Mix together all ingredients and refrigerate overnight.

Cynthia Koch
NSO Women's Committee Member

Cocktail Salt Sticks

MAKES 4 DOZEN

½ pound farmer's cheese

½ pound all-purpose flour

½ pound unsalted butter

Egg wash of 1 egg yolk and 1 tablespoon water

Salt, to sprinkle on top, optional

Caraway seeds, optional

Mix ingredients together in a food processor or by hand.

Roll out ¾ inch thick and cut in lengths (any size desired). Brush with egg wash. Sprinkle with salt and caraway seeds, if desired.

Bake in preheated 400 degree oven for 15 minutes or until brown on top.

Keep in tin; can be frozen and reheated in 350 degree oven.

Ingrid Monaghan
Former NSO FANS Member

HOT APPETIZERS

Mousseline St. Jacques

MAKES 12 APPETIZERS

1 pound scallops

1 pint heavy cream, whipped

Salt and freshly ground pepper

12 large leaves of Boston lettuce

½ cup julienne of carrots

½ cup julienne of celery

½ cup fresh, diced tomatoes

2 tablespoons julienne of truffles

½ pound sweet butter

2 egg yolks

2 tablespoons chopped shallots

½ cup white wine

½ cup fish stock

Purée scallops in food processor. Add cream and mix. Season mousseline with salt and pepper.

Blanch lettuce leaves. Cool and drain on napkin. Stuff lettuce leaves with mousseline and wrap.

Cook julienne of carrots and celery. Peel and seed tomatoes. Then dice. Prepare julienne of truffles.

To prepare hollandaise, clarify butter. Whip egg yolks on top of double boiler. Then add clarified butter.

Combine shallots, white wine and fish stock in saucepan. Bring to a boil and add mousseline. Cook for 5 minutes. Remove mousseline from cooking juice. Reduce cooking juice to half. Add carrots and celery juilienne, tomatoes, and truffles. Cook for 2 more minutes. Add hollandaise and mix together. Season to taste.

To serve, pour sauce on bottom of platter and place mousseline on top.

Chef Jean-Pierre Goyenvalle
Le Lion d'Or Restaurant

Pirozhki

MAKES 75 TURNOVERS

DOUGH
10 ounces evaporated milk

½ cup warm water

4 eggs

½ pound butter

½ pound margarine

2 packets dry yeast plus 2 teaspoons sugar

1 teaspoon salt

6½ cups all-purpose flour

FILLING
¾ pound lean ground beef

2 large onions, chopped

4 hard-boiled eggs, chopped

2 tablespoons finely chopped dill, fresh or 1 tablespoon dry dill weed

Salt, freshly ground pepper to taste

DOUGH
Proof yeast; in large glass measuring cup or pan, mix sugar and yeast. Add warm water and stir to dissolve. Put in warm place to rise. In a large bowl, mix butter, margarine (softened), 3 eggs and evaporated milk well with hands. Add yeast mixture. Add flour and salt. Mix thoroughly until smooth and elastic (about 5 minutes). Wrap in floured foil and place on a large bread board or platter and refrigerate overnight or at least 8 hours.

FILLING
Sauté beef in small quantities until just brown. Put in a large bowl and tilt bowl to side to drain off fat. Remove fat. Sauté chopped onion in one stick of butter until transparent. Add to beef. Add finely chopped eggs, dill, salt and pepper. Mix well. Chill.

ASSEMBLY
Divide dough into quarters. Roll dough ¼ inch thick, one quarter of dough at a time. Cut in 2½-inch squares. Place a heaping teaspoonful of filling in center and bring corners together to make a square pillow shape. Crimp seams tightly. Place one inch apart on ungreased cookie sheets. Chill for 30 minutes. Brush with egg wash made by beating 1 egg with 1 teaspoon of water. Bake in a 425 degree oven for 20 to 25 minutes.

Can be made ahead and frozen. Will keep up to six months in a freezer. To freeze; cool thoroughly; freeze in heavy duty freezer bags. Reheat in foil-lined baking pan in one layer for 25 minutes in a 375 degree oven.

Serve warm with cocktails, or as an accompaniment to soup or consommé.

Galina Vishnevskaya
Soprano, Guest Artist

Pierogis

Serves 4 to 6

Dough
2 cups flour

1 large egg

½ teaspoon salt

⅓–½ cup water

Filling
1 cup hot mashed potatoes

½ cup grated cheese, extra sharp

1 beaten egg

½ teaspoon salt

¼ teaspoon freshly ground pepper

Mix flour, egg and salt. Stir in water to form stiff dough. Divide in half, and roll paper thin. Cut circles with a large biscuit cutter. Set aside while making filling.

Mix potatoes, grated cheese, egg, salt and pepper. Fill each circle with heaping teaspoon of filling. Fold in half, moisten edge with water and press to seal.

Drop in boiling, salted water and cook 3 to 5 minutes (they will start to rise to top of water). Remove with slotted spoon. Place in single layer on serving dish.

Serve by pouring melted butter over top or with sour cream on the side. Can be kept in a 300 degree oven, covered with foil, for up to an hour. Uncooked pierogis may be frozen or refrigerated several hours ahead.

Sandy Wheeler
Former NSO FANS Member

Slava's Siberian Pelmeni

SERVES 4 AS A MAIN COURSE

SERVES 6 AS A FIRST COURSE

Pelmeni have been made in Siberia for centuries and frozen in the snow outside the house. Travelers would carry them frozen; then cook them in melted snow over a campfire.

DOUGH
4-4½ cups flour

1 whole egg

1 egg yolk

Salad oil to make 1 cup liquid with eggs

1 cup water

FILLING
½ large onion

2 cloves garlic

¾ pound lean ground beef

½ pound lean ground pork

½ teaspoon freshly ground pepper

Salt to taste

¼ cup water

Melted butter

OPTIONAL
Sour cream

Freshly ground black pepper

Vinegar

Soy sauce

DOUGH

Make a well in center of flour. Measure eggs and oil to make 1 cup and add to well. Add water; then mix thoroughly until dough can be gathered into a compact ball. Knead, folding over until dough is smooth and elastic. Refrigerate for at least 1 hour, wrapped in slightly floured wax paper.

FILLING

Chop onion and garlic very finely and mix with meat, pepper, salt and water. Meat mixture should be light and fluffy. If heavy and dense, add more water. Mix thoroughly.

Roll out dough, one quarter at a time, until almost paper-thin. To keep dough from sticking and shrinking during rolling, make a quarter turn every 5 or 6 rolls.

Cut out 1¾-inch circles of dough with a biscuit cutter. Put a teaspoon of filling in center, fold over edges, and crimp together firmly with fingers. Then bring together corners of finished semi-circle, making a triangular pouch. Store finished raw pelmeni on 3 well-floured cookie sheets. Pelmeni can be frozen or cooked at this point.

To cook, place pelmeni (25 to 30 at a time) into 6 quarts of well-salted, boiling water. Stir carefully to prevent sticking at the bottom. Cook 3 minutes, timing when pelmeni start rising.

Remove from boiling water with slotted spoon. Sprinkle lightly with melted butter, and serve with all or any of the following: sour cream, freshly ground black pepper, vinegar or soy sauce.

Mstislav Rostropovich
NSO Conductor Laureate
NSO Music Director
1970-1977

Chicken Liver Strudel

MAKES 18 TO 24 SLICES

1 medium onion, finely chopped

6 tablespoons butter

1 pound chicken livers

¼ pound fresh mushrooms, sliced

2 tablespoons cognac

¼ cup soft bread crumbs

Salt and pepper to taste

1 egg, lightly beaten

⅛ teaspoon allspice

2 tablespoons fresh parsley, chopped

¼ pound (approximately) phyllo dough sheets (10 sheets)

Melted butter

Preheat oven to 350 degrees. In a small skillet, sauté the onion in 2 tablespoons of butter, until tender and transparent; do not brown. Add remaining butter and liver. Cook quickly until browned on all sides. Add mushrooms and cook 3 minutes more.

Turn liver mixture onto a chopping board and chop until fairly fine. Scrape into a bowl and add cognac, bread crumbs, salt, pepper, egg, allspice and parsley. Mix. Allow to cool. Take two sheets of phyllo and brush with melted butter. Repeat with 10 sheets. Mold liver mixture into a sausage and place along phyllo. Roll the phyllo up and place on a greased baking sheet and bake until crispy and golden, about 30 to 40 minutes.

You may serve the strudel immediately or let it cool and wrap in aluminum foil to freeze. When ready to use, remove from freezer and thaw for 20 minutes. Slice, with a serrated knife, into pieces ½ inch long. Bake in a preheated oven at 375 degrees for 15 minutes.

Miriam Benbassat

Dolmadakia Avgolemono (Stuffed Grape Leaves with Egg and Lemon Sauce)

MAKES 35 TO 40 PIECES

1 pound ground beef

½ pound ground pork

¼ cup rice

1 whole egg

3 egg yolks

½ cup peeled tomatoes

8 ounces grape leaves

1 medium onion, grated

¼ bunch parsley

¼ bunch dill

½ cup butter

2 ounces flour

Salt and freshly ground pepper

1 ounce chicken bouillon

3 lemons

To prepare the stuffed grape leaves, boil water in a large saucepan and add leaves (unrolled). Allow water to come to a second boil; then place under cold running water. Remove leaves when they are cold and stack them by hand, one by one, into a loose pile.

Put both ground meats in a large bowl; add whole egg, rice, onion, tomatoes (cut into small pieces), liquid from chopped tomato, finely chopped parsley and dill, salt and pepper to taste and a cup of water (or, if available, a cup of beef or chicken broth instead of water).

Knead all ingredients in bowl together. Spread leaves, one by one, on a flat surface and wrap each one around meat mixture, allowing a heaping tablespoonful or more for each. (Note: before wrapping, stalk of each leaf should be cut off. The leaf should be wrapped around stuffing so that shiny side of leaf is on outside.)

Place stuffed vine leaves one by one into a large saucepan, cover with ½ lemon cut into thin slices, and weight them down with a plate placed over top of contents. In another saucepan, boil enough water to cover leaves. Pour over leaves, together with chicken bouillon.

Cover saucepan and simmer slowly for 2 hours, adding more liquid if necessary.

Remove saucepan from heat and drain remaining liquid (to be used in making egg and lemon sauce).

EGG AND LEMON SAUCE

Melt butter in a saucepan, add flour and stir for a few minutes with a wooden spoon. Add liquid from vine leaves, after it has

continued...

cooled to lukewarm. Stir with a wire whisk until it forms a smooth paste and allow to boil slowly over low heat, stirring from time to time for about 5 minutes. (Care must be taken not to cook mixture at too high heat.)

Remove from heat and allow to cool. Beat juice of remaining lemons with 3 egg yolks and add sauce little by little. Strain sauce and cover it, leaving in a warm place.

To serve, place hot stuffed leaves on a platter and pour warm sauce over. Dolmadakia are eaten hot and may be served as a first or main course. They are also often served as cocktail snacks. Sauce may be adjusted, if too thick, with broth and water or a little milk or, if too runny, with a little corn starch.

The Embassy of Greece

Blini

Makes 24 to 36 pieces

This classic recipe is similar to the blini served at the former landmark Russian Tea Room in New York.

2½ cups lukewarm milk

1 tablespoon (1 envelope) dry yeast

1 cup white flour, sifted

1 cup buckwheat flour, sifted

3 tablespoons sugar

½ teaspoon salt

6 tablespoons unsalted butter, melted and cooled

3 eggs, lightly beaten

Melted butter for frying

In a small bowl combine the milk and yeast and whisk to dissolve. In a large bowl, combine both flours, sugar and salt. Beat in each addition with a wire whisk; add milk mixture, butter and the eggs. Beat until smooth. Cover bowl with cloth or plastic and set in a larger bowl containing warm water. Put in a warm, draft-free place and let rise for 60 to 90 minutes, or until double in bulk.

Preheat oven to 200 degrees. Preheat crêpe pan or griddle over medium heat and brush very lightly with melted butter. Pour about 3 tablespoons of the batter onto the crêpe pan and fry until golden brown on both sides. Brush pan with butter as needed. Put prepared blini in pan covered by kitchen towels and keep them in the oven while remainder are being fried.

Serve with melted butter, sour cream, caviar or smoked fish.

Sonia Peterson

Jewish Pizza

SERVES 6 TO 8

⅓ cup sour cream or crème fraiche

3 tablespoons minced shallots or scallions

2 tablespoons minced fresh dill

1½ tablespoons fresh lemon juice

Salt and pepper to taste

3 cups grated potato (use a starchy type, such as Russet)

½ stick of butter, melted

1 tablespoon flour

½ pound smoked salmon/lox

Red or black caviar for garnish

Squirt of lemon juice to taste

Combine sour cream or crème fraiche, shallots or scallions, dill, lemon, salt and pepper. Cover and refrigerate.

Combine grated potato, melted butter and flour in a large bowl. In a 10-inch ovenproof skillet (preferably cast iron), sprinkle potato mixture in pan over medium heat and press down with a spatula to flatten. Cook approximately 4 minutes until potato holds together like a latke.

Place a 10-inch plate over the skillet and invert onto plate. Then slide potato back onto skillet and cook 4 more minutes on opposite side. Place into preheated oven at 425 degrees for approximately 10 minutes or until crisp.

Move potato pancake to platter, and spread with sour cream mixture. Cover with smoked salmon and garnishes. Season with lemon juice. Cut into pizza wedges with wheel type cutter.

Matthew Guilford
NSO Bass Trombone

Quiche

SERVES 8

CRUST

1 cup flour

1 egg yolk

7 tablespoons butter, room temperature

Pinch salt

1 tablespoon water
(add last)

QUICHE FILLING

8 strips bacon, crisp and chopped

1 cup Gruyère cheese, cubed (approximately ¾ pound)

⅓ cup Parmesan cheese

4 eggs

2 cups (1 pint) heavy whipping cream, whipped

¼ teaspoon nutmeg

½ teaspoon salt

¼ teaspoon freshly ground black pepper

¼ teaspoon freshly ground white pepper

For more even, blind baking (prebaking of pie shells) use dried beans on top of parchment paper. Before baking pie shells, prick crust with fork.

CRUST

Knead all ingredients with hands in a bowl until it forms a ball. Add water last. Refrigerate in wax paper. Preheat oven to 375 degrees. Roll out. Bake for 13 minutes. Use beans in bottom of quiche dish to hold down crust. It is better to make the crust one day ahead. It keeps well in the refrigerator for one week.

QUICHE FILLING

Preheat oven to 350 degrees. Put cheeses and bacon in bottom of crust. May be made ahead up to this point. Beat eggs and add all the seasonings. Beat more. Add cream and bake for one hour at 350 degrees.

—

Susan Porter
NSO Board Member

Puffed Cheese Hors d'Oeuvres

MAKES 36 PIECES

8-ounce package cream cheese

1 egg yolk

½ teaspoon grated onion

¼ teaspoon salt

9 slices firm white bread

6 tablespoons butter

Preheat oven to 325 degrees. Blend cheese thoroughly with egg yolk, onion, and salt. Chill.

Cut 4 rounds from each slice of bread with round cookie cutter. Brush both sides of bread with melted butter. Place on a cookie sheet. Bake 5 to 7 minutes at 325 degrees until bottoms are very light brown. Turn and do same to other side.

Cover entire top of bread rounds with cheese mixture, rounding a little on top. (At this point, rounds can be frozen individually on a cookie sheet and when well frozen placed in a plastic bag.)

Bake at 325 degrees for 5 minutes and then place under broiler for 2 to 3 minutes until light brown. Serve hot.

Barbara Phillips
Former NSO FANS Member

Gougères (Cheese Puffs)

MAKES ABOUT 25 PIECES

½ cup water

1¼ cups flour

½ cup butter

4 eggs

½ teaspoon salt

4½ ounces Gruyère cheese, grated

Bring water, butter and salt to a boil. Add the flour and stir over a low heat until the dough forms a ball. Remove from heat. Place the dough in a bowl and incorporate the eggs one at a time. Add the Gruyère cheese, cut into very small cubes or grated. Place teaspoonfuls of dough on a greased baking tray and bake for 20 to 25 minutes in an oven set at 450 degrees.

Laurent Weibel
NSO Second Violin

Spinach Balls

SERVES 12 TO 18

2 10-ounce packages chopped spinach

3 cups herb-seasoned Pepperidge Farm stuffing mix

1 medium onion, finely chopped

6 eggs, well beaten

¾ cup butter, melted

½ cup Parmesan cheese, grated

1 teaspoon black pepper

1½ teaspoons garlic salt

½ teaspoon dried thyme

Cook spinach according to package directions and drain very well, removing all moisture. Combine with other ingredients and mix well. Shape into small balls and place on a lightly greased cookie sheet. Bake at 325 degrees for 15 to 20 minutes.

May be made ahead of time and frozen, but thaw at least partly before baking. You may need to increase baking time.

—
Farinelli Family

Onion Canapé

SERVES 8

1 loaf of fresh bread (white, rye or both), sliced into rounds

1 large Bermuda, Vidalia or sweet onion, thinly sliced into rounds

½ cup mayonnaise

¼ cup Parmesan cheese, grated

Paprika to taste

Place a thin round of onion on each fresh round of bread. Spread 1 teaspoon of mayonnaise on top of each round. Sprinkle ½ teaspoon of grated Parmesan cheese on top of mayonnaise. Sprinkle lightly with paprika to taste. Place under broiler until a golden brown. Watch canapés carefully, as they brown quickly if the broiler is too hot.

You can also add Guldens dark mustard to the mixture.

—
Katie Tardio
NSO Women's Committee Member

Blackeyed Pea Dip

SERVES 12

This recipe was served on April 22, 1999 at a reception at the home of NSO National Trustee Doyce Hancock Deas, honoring the National Symphony Orchestra's Residency in Mississippi.

1 15-ounce can of black eyed peas

1 teaspoon seasoned salt

2 tablespoons minced onion

1 tablespoon diced jalapeño pepper

1½ cups grated sharp cheddar cheese

¼ cup butter

1 3-ounce can deviled ham

4 ounces mozzarella cheese

Cook peas for two minutes and drain. Mash lightly with a fork. Mix with salt, minced onion, diced jalapeño pepper, sharp cheddar cheese, butter and deviled ham. Pour into a 9-inch round baking dish. Top with mozzarella cheese. Bake at 350 degrees for 20 minutes or until thoroughly heated.

Doyce Hancock Deas
NSO National Trustee

Deviled Crab

SERVES 6

2 tablespoons onion, finely chopped

½ cup green pepper, finely chopped

¼ cup butter

¼ cup flour

1 cup light cream

1 teaspoon Worcestershire sauce

1 teaspoon lemon juice

¼ teaspoon salt

¼ teaspoon black pepper

¼ teaspoon dry mustard

2 to 3 drops hot pepper sauce

Dash cayenne pepper

2 7½-ounce cans crabmeat, drained and flaked

2 eggs, hard cooked, finely diced

⅓ cup fresh bread crumbs

Watercress sprigs

6 ramekins or clam baking shells

Sauté the 2 tablespoons finely chopped onion and the finely chopped green pepper in 2 tablespoons butter until soft. Add remaining 2 tablespoons butter. Sprinkle in ¼ cup flour, stirring well. Cook for 30 seconds. Gradually stir in one cup light cream. Add 1 teaspoon each Worcestershire sauce and lemon juice, ¼ teaspoon each salt, black pepper, dry mustard, 2 to 3 drops hot pepper sauce and a dash of cayenne pepper. Cook gently, stirring, until sauce boils and thickens.

Add 2 cans crabmeat, drained and flaked, to sauce. Heat 3 minutes more. Stir in finely diced, hard cooked eggs. Divide mixture between six individual ramekins or clam baking shells. Allow ½ cup per serving. Sprinkle each with 1 tablespoon fresh bread crumbs. Bake 8 to 10 minutes at 450 degrees or until crumbs are browned. Garnish with watercress sprigs.

Nancy Pittman
NSO Women's Committee Member

Hot Crab Dip

SERVES 12

1 pound crabmeat

2 8-ounce packages cream cheese

½ pint sour cream

4 heaping teaspoons mayonnaise

1 teaspoon Worcestershire sauce

1 teaspoon dry mustard

1 teaspoon garlic salt

½ lemon squeezed

3 tablespoons sherry

TOPPING
½ cup cheddar cheese, grated

Combine above ingredients, folding in crabmeat last. Spread cheese topping on top before baking. Bake in 13x9-inch serving dish at 325 degrees for 30 minutes. Can be made ahead of time and refrigerated before baking.

Anna Pfeiffer
NSO Board Member

Roast Pork Appetizer

SERVES 6

1 pound pork shoulder

1 tablespoon rice wine

1 tablespoon soy sauce

1 teaspoon salt

1 tablespoon sugar

1 tablespoon hoisin sauce (plum sauce)

¼ teaspoon five-spice powder

3 cloves mashed garlic

2 ounces tomato color

Rinse the meat, drain and pat dry. Combine all of the other ingredients in a large bowl. Place the meat in the large bowl and cover with the mixture of all of the ingredients. Marinate the meat for at least 2 hours. Spoon marinade over meat frequently so meat will marinate evenly.

Preheat the oven to 450 degrees. Pour one cup of water in a large shallow roasting pan, then place on lowest rack of oven to collect the drippings.

Bake for 30 minutes, basting occasionally. To test for doneness, prick the meat with a fork. If the resulting liquid is clear, the roast pork is done.

Thinly slice and serve.

Larry La
Meiwah Restaurant

The National Symphony Orchestra performs in the Musikvereinsaal,
Vienna, Austria (1982). Credit Jack Buxbaum.

Note: *recipes marked with this icon are from the original National Symphony Orchestra*
Cookbook, published by FANS (Friends Assisting the National Symphony) in 1983.

Soups

COLD SOUPS

Chilled Cucumber Soup

SERVES 4

3 large cucumbers, peeled, seeded and chopped

1 cup plain yogurt

1 clove garlic

⅔ cup sour cream

2 tablespoons fresh dill

Salt and freshly ground pepper to taste

Paprika, for garnish

Place all ingredients except paprika into a food processor; beat until smooth.

Chill. Serve with additional minced dill and paprika for garnish. Soup can be made in advance.

Mrs. Harry E. Gould, Jr.

Cold Cucumber Soup

SERVES 6

3 medium cucumbers

½ cup chopped onion

2 tablespoons butter

2 cups chicken broth

1 tablespoon flour

1 teaspoon Lawry's salt

1 cup sour cream (can use 40% reduced fat sour cream if preferred)

¾ tablespoon lemon juice

⅛ teaspoon dried dill

Sprigs of fresh dill

Pare and slice 2 cucumbers. Cook with onions in butter until softened. Stir in flour. Add broth. Cover and simmer until they are soft and tender. Purée until smooth in blender. Add seasoned salt, lemon juice and dill. Chill soup for 4 hours.

Pare remaining cucumber; cut in half lengthwise and scoop out seeds. Grate medium coarse. Add to chilled soup with sour cream. Garnish each bowl with dill sprigs.

Ann Friedman
NSO Board Member

Gazpacho

SERVES 6

2 large tomatoes, peeled

1 large cucumber, peeled

1 medium onion

1 medium green pepper

24 ounces Sacramento tomato juice

¼ cup olive oil

⅓ cup red wine vinegar

¼ teaspoon Tabasco

⅛ teaspoon black pepper, coarsely ground

1½ teaspoons salt

Croutons

Use blender or food processor to combine all solid ingredients and blend with some of tomato juice until puréed. Add remaining ingredients and rest of tomato juice. Chill for 2 hours. You can reserve some of the vegetables, chop them up and use to garnish soup along with freshly toasted croutons.

This is easy to take to a picnic and serve in plastic cups.

Mrs. Edison W. Dick

White Gazpacho

SERVES 4

1½ large cucumbers, peeled

1 garlic clove

1 14-ounce can chicken broth

10½ ounces sour cream

1 teaspoon wine vinegar

3 teaspoons lemon juice

¼ teaspoon Tabasco sauce

1½ teaspoons pepper

GARNISH

Tomatoes

Green peppers

Cucumbers

Blend all ingredients except the cucumbers together in a blender and pour into a container. Then purée the cucumbers and add to gazpacho.

GARNISH

Using the julienne blade of a food processor, slice up tomatoes, green peppers and cucumbers and use as a garnish, or chop by hand (the texture is better this way).

Cookbook Committee

Cold Zucchini Soup

SERVES 4

2 tablespoons butter

2 tablespoons finely chopped shallots

1 clove garlic, minced

1 pound zucchini, cleaned and sliced thin (do not peel)

1 teaspoon curry or to taste

1 teaspoon salt

1 cup cream (light or heavy)

1¾ cups chicken broth, preferably homemade

In a skillet heat butter and add shallots, garlic and zucchini. Cover pan and simmer ingredients for about 10 minutes. Stir every few minutes. Do not let brown. Cool.

Place mixture in blender and add curry, salt, cream and broth. Blend mixture 1 minute and chill.

Laurie G. Firestone
Former NSO Board Member

Cold Spinach Soup

SERVES 6

1 package frozen, chopped spinach, cooked

4 cups light cream

4 chicken bouillon cubes

¼ cup dry vermouth

½ teaspoon ground mace, optional

1 tablespoon grated lemon rind

Salt and pepper to taste

2 hard-boiled eggs (chopped)

Croutons

Put cooked spinach into blender and reduce to pulp.

Put bouillon cubes into cream and scald, stirring until cubes are dissolved. (I put cream in top of double-boiler; it is easier and keeps it from burning!!) Remove from heat. Stir in spinach, vermouth, lemon rind and mace. Add salt and pepper to taste. Chill. Top with eggs or serve piping hot with croutons.

Mrs. Barbara Bush
Former First Lady

HOT SOUPS

Minestra Genovese di Fagiolini al Pesto (Bean Soup with Pesto)

SERVES 8

Fresh basil is a must for pesto.

Soup
2 cups dried navy beans

2½ quarts water

1½ cups peeled, diced potatoes

1 stalk celery, diced

1 large leek, sliced

1 cup grated carrots

1½ teaspoons salt

½ teaspoon freshly ground pepper

2 slices cooked bacon, chopped small

1 cup uncooked noodles

PESTO
1 cup fresh basil leaves

½ bunch parsley without stems

½ cup pine nuts or almonds

2 garlic cloves, peeled

¾ cup freshly grated Parmesan cheese

½ cup olive oil

Soup
Soak beans in cold water for 1 hour. Drain. Cook beans in 2½ quarts water for 2½ hours.

Add vegetables, salt and pepper; continue simmering for 30 minutes. Add bacon and cook for 10 minutes more. Add noodles and cook until al dente. While soup is cooking make pesto sauce.

Blend all pesto ingredients in a blender or food processor, adding olive oil last. Dribble olive oil.

Combine pesto with soup and serve immediately.

Joan C-C Oppenheimer

Pesto Minestrone Soup

SERVES 8

1 onion

6 sage leaves

1 rosemary sprig

½ cup extra virgin olive oil

1 package dried porcini mushrooms, soaked in water

4 ounces cabbage

1 stalk celery

1 leek

1 cup peas

1 zucchini

1 handful parsley leaves

1 carrot

3 ounces string beans, cut into small pieces

1 can canellini beans, drained and washed (if you use dried they must soak overnight)

1½ cups arborio rice

8 cups chicken broth

½ cup basil leaves

1 tablespoon Pecorino cheese, grated

2 tablespoons Parmesan cheese, grated

2 garlic cloves

¼ cup pine nuts

Salt to taste

In a food processor, chop the onion, sage and rosemary. Stir fry with 2 tablespoons of the oil in a large stockpot. Roughly dice all the vegetables and add them to the pot. Stir fry for about 10 minutes. Add the chicken broth, salt and bring to a boil. Cook for 2½ hours over low heat. Add the rice and cook ½ hour more.

Process the basil with the remaining oil, Pecorino cheese, Parmesan cheese, garlic and pine nuts. Pour the minestrone in a soup tureen. Add the basil mixture, stir and serve.

—

Susan Porter
NSO Board Member

Minestra di Pasta e Fagioli

SERVES 6

¾ cup dried borlotti beans, soaked overnight, drained and rinsed

1 medium potato, roughly chopped

1 celery stalk, roughly chopped

1 small carrot, roughly chopped

1 fresh bay leaf

1 fresh sage leaf

1 fresh rosemary sprig

1 garlic clove

1 shallot, chopped

¼ pound pancetta or slab bacon

Salt and pepper

4 tablespoons extra virgin olive oil

In a large stockpot, add the extra virgin olive oil, pancetta combined with the beans, vegetables, herbs, garlic, shallots and 1 quart of water. Bring to a boil and cook covered over very low heat for about 1 hour. Cook until the beans are very tender.

Taste the soup and adjust the seasoning with salt and freshly ground black pepper. Add extra virgin olive oil to each serving as desired.

Domenico Cornacchia
Café Milano

Avgolemono (Chicken with Rice Soup)

SERVES 8

7 cups chicken broth

½ cup long grain rice

Salt and freshly ground pepper to taste

6 large eggs, beaten

½ cup strained lemon juice

Chopped fresh parsley leaves for decoration, optional

Heat chicken broth almost to a rolling state and slowly pour in rice, stirring to prevent sticking. Lower heat to slow roll. Caution: continue stirring and watch carefully until certain that soup will not overflow.

When rice is almost cooked, beat eggs well. Slowly add lemon juice to eggs and blend well. Continue beating egg and lemon mixture while adding about 1½ cups of hot soup to it. Pour this mixture back into soup kettle, stirring constantly to prevent curdling. Serve immediately.

Garnish with parsley, if desired.

Mrs. Tas Coroneos

Chicken Vegetable Soup

SERVES 6 TO 8

4 cups homemade chicken broth

2 chicken breast halves, boned and skinned

1 cup onions, diced

1 cup carrots, diced

1 cup leeks, white only, diced

1 cup celery, diced

½ cup dry white vermouth or dry white wine

1 bay leaf

Salt and freshly ground white pepper

RICE AND ONION SOUP PURÉE

2 cups onions, sliced

2 tablespoons butter

4 cups chicken broth

½ cup raw white rice

Salt and freshly ground white pepper

In a medium size soup pot, bring 4 cups of chicken broth to simmer. Add chicken breast, vegetables, wine and bay leaf. Let it simmer for 5 minutes. Remove the chicken breasts and let the vegetables continue to simmer while you julienne the chicken. Add julienned chicken back to the pot and cook 5 minutes more.

Turn off heat and let chicken steep in the soup for 15 minutes. Correct seasonings.

Assemble purée: In a sautéuse, sauté the sliced onions slowly in the butter until tender. Add the raw rice. Add 4 cups of chicken broth and stir. Cover and simmer for 20 minutes or until the rice is tender.

Purée the rice mixture in a food processor until you have a creamy thickened purée. Add purée to chicken vegetable pot and stir. Heat and soup is ready to serve.

Cookbook Committee

Lentil Soup

SERVES 10 TO 12

2 cups dried lentils

2½ quarts water

2 tablespoons cooking oil

¾ cup chopped carrots

¾ cup chopped onions

¾ cup chopped celery

2 cloves garlic, minced

1 bay leaf

2 whole cloves

Dash cayenne pepper

1 teaspoon salt

¼ teaspoon black pepper

15 or 16-ounce can of tomatoes, cut up

1 tablespoon Worcestershire sauce

½ teaspoon dried thyme

½ to 1 pound fully cooked smoked sausage links, sliced

Rinse lentils; set aside. In a large soup kettle cook carrots, onions, celery and garlic in the hot oil until tender but not brown. Tie the bay leaf and cloves in cheesecloth. Stir in the lentils, water, undrained tomatoes, Worcestershire sauce, thyme, salt, pepper and the cheesecloth bundle. Bring to boil; reduce heat and simmer for 1½ hours, stirring occasionally. Add sausage slices and simmer for an additional ½ hour. Discard cheesecloth. Taste to correct seasonings. You may need to add additional salt and pepper. Garnish each serving with freshly snipped parsley.

Jane Gough
NSO Women's Committee Member

Heavenly Carrot Soup

SERVES 6

1 cup chopped onion

4 tablespoons butter

½ cup dry white wine

1 pound carrots, finely chopped

1½ teaspoons ground coriander

4 cups chicken broth

Salt and freshly ground pepper to taste

In a large, heavy saucepan, sauté onion in butter until soft. Add wine and carrots. Cover tightly, and cook over very low heat for 30 minutes. Check a couple times, stirring to keep from browning (although a little bit adds something).

Place carrot mixture in electric blender with coriander and some of chicken broth. Purée, then return to saucepan and whisk in remaining broth and salt and pepper to taste. Serve hot, cold, or at room temperature. If serving hot, reheat but do not boil.

Cookbook Committee

Onion Soup

SERVES 6 TO 8

1½ pounds yellow onions

Oil and butter as needed

2 cloves garlic, crushed

4 tablespoons butter

2 quarts beef stock or 4 10-ounce cans plus 1 cup of water

1 teaspoon salt (omit if using canned stock)

Pinch sugar

1 teaspoon dried mustard

1 bay leaf

1½ teaspoons sage

1 cup dry red wine

Salt and freshly ground pepper to taste

GRATINÉE

Slightly dry French bread

Oil or butter

1½ cups grated cheese (Swiss, Gruyère, Parmesan)

Peel onions; slice very thin. Melt oil and butter together in a very heavy 3-quart saucepan. Toss onions and garlic in melted fat to coat thoroughly; cook covered over medium heat until very tender. Uncover, add sugar and raise heat. Stir frequently to prevent sticking or burning; cook until onions are a deep caramel color.

Heat 2 cups of stock or stock and water to boiling; add slowly to onions, stirring vigorously. When this mixture is well blended, add rest of liquids and seasonings except salt and pepper. Bring to a boil, reduce heat and simmer covered for 35 to 40 minutes, stirring occasionally. Correct seasoning, but do not oversalt if serving soup with a strong cheese.

Slice bread about 1 inch thick, enough to cover surface of an ovenproof baking dish or casserole, or to fit snugly in individual ovenproof bowls. Lightly butter or oil both sides and toast to a light brown on both sides. Bring soup to a simmer and ladle it into serving vessel or bowls. Top with toasted bread, covering as much of surface as possible; then spread cheese on top. Sprinkle a little oil over cheese and place in middle of a 350 degree oven for 30 minutes. The cheese should be slowly bubbling.

Francine Morris Swift
Former NSO FANS Member

Red and Yellow Bell Pepper Soup

SERVES 6

¼ cup butter

1 large onion, chopped

2 cloves garlic, crushed

8 ounces tomatoes, coarsely chopped

8 ounces red bell peppers, seeded, chopped (2)

4-5 cups vegetable stock

8 ounces yellow bell peppers, seeded, chopped (2)

1 tablespoon arrowroot

Salt and pepper to taste

Blanched almonds or pine nuts

2 slices white bread, crust removed

½ cup half and half

Place half of butter, half of onion and 1 garlic clove in a large saucepan. Place remaining butter, onion and garlic in another large saucepan. Gently cook both until onion is soft. Add tomatoes, red bell peppers and half of stock to one pan. Add yellow bell peppers and remaining stock to other pan. Simmer both mixtures 20 minutes.

In a food processor fitted with a metal blade or a blender, process one mixture to a purée. Press purée through a sieve set over a bowl. Clean pan and return purée to clean pan. Repeat procedure with remaining mixture. Season both purées with salt and pepper. In a small bowl, blend arrowroot with a small amount of water and stir into red bell pepper mixture. Reheat to thicken.

In food processor fitted with a metal blade or blender, process almonds, bread and half and half to a purée. Stir into yellow bell pepper purée and reheat. Pour each soup into a pitcher. Pour soups into individual bowls, pouring red bell pepper soup from one side and yellow bell pepper soup from opposite side. Serve at once. Do not dilute stock too much, especially when preparing the red pepper soup. Serve lukewarm.

Cookbook Committee

Sylvia's Quick Curried Pea Soup

SERVES 4

1 10-ounce package of frozen peas

1 medium onion, sliced

1 carrot, sliced

1 clove garlic

1 stalk of celery with leaves

1 medium potato

1 teaspoon curry

2 cups chicken broth

1 cup light cream

Simmer ingredients in 1½ cups of chicken broth until soft. Blend in a blender until smooth. Add remaining ½ cup of chicken broth. Add the light cream to taste.

Sylvia Alimena
NSO Horn

Potato, Carrot and Leek Soup

SERVES 8 TO 10

1 pound peeled Yukon gold potatoes, sliced

1 pound thinly sliced leek, including tender green

1 or 2 carrots, sliced

2 quarts water and/or chicken broth

1 tablespoon salt

3 tablespoons minced parsley

Combine potatoes, leek, carrots, water or chicken broth and salt in a large pot. Simmer for one hour partially covered. Remove soup from pot and purée in a blender. Sprinkle with parsley before serving.

Alice Kogan Weinreb
NSO Flute

Pumpkin Soup

SERVES 6

4 green onions and tops, thinly sliced

1 onion, thinly sliced

4 tablespoons butter, melted

5 cups chicken stock

½ teaspoon garlic powder

1 cup whipping cream

½ cup heavy cream, whipped

2 carrots, sliced

1 29-ounce can pumpkin

Salt to taste

2 tablespoons flour

½ cup tiny homemade croutons

Sauté all the onions and carrots in 3 tablespoons butter until soft. Add the pumpkin and stock; blend well. Add salt to taste and garlic powder. Simmer about 25 minutes. Mix the flour and 1 tablespoon softened butter. Stir into soup. Bring to boil. Remove from heat and purée in blender or food processor. Add the cream. Return to heat and bring to boil. If served cold, chill thoroughly. Garnish with whipped cream and croutons.

Nancy Peery Marriott
NSO Board Member

Pumpkin Soup with Ham

SERVES 6

1 medium onion, chopped

2 tablespoons butter

3 cups canned pumpkin

2 14-ounce cans chicken broth

2 tablespoons brown sugar

2 bay leaves

¼ teaspoon nutmeg

¼ teaspoon freshly ground pepper

1 cup heavy cream

1 cup ham, finely chopped, optional

1 tablespoon oil, optional

Cook onion in butter until tender. Stir in pumpkin, chicken broth, brown sugar, bay leaves, nutmeg and pepper. Bring to a boil. Reduce heat and simmer, covered, for 10 minutes. Discard bay leaves. Stir in the heavy cream. Process until smooth. Reheat. If desired, cook the ham in oil in a skillet for 10 minutes or until crisp. Drain. Serve the ham over the soup.

Cheris Garrison
NSO Women's Committee Member

Tomato Basil Soup

SERVES 6

5 tablespoons olive oil

2 medium sweet onions

2 teaspoons kosher salt

Pepper to taste

29 ounces canned tomatoes, drained, reserving juice

3 tablespoons sugar

Fresh chopped basil to taste (½–1 cup)

Sweat onion in oil for 5 minutes until translucent. Add drained tomatoes and sugar. Cook for 5 minutes. Add juice from tomatoes and water to comprise 4 cups of liquid. Simmer for 15 minutes, stirring often. Remove from heat and add basil. Let rest for 10 minutes. Purée and adjust seasoning. Serve hot or cold. Better if served next day. Adjust seasoning again before serving.

Jane de Lange
NSO Women's Committee Member

The National Symphony Orchestra in the Kennedy Center Concert Hall with Music Director Antal Doráti (1970s). Photo from NSO Archives.

Note: *recipes marked with this icon are from the original National Symphony Orchestra Cookbook, published by FANS (Friends Assisting the National Symphony) in 1983.*

Egg & Cheese Dishes

EGG & CHEESE DISHES

Spinach Roll with Ham

SERVES 4 TO 6

1 pound fresh spinach

6 eggs, separated

¼ pound butter

3 tablespoons flour

1 tablespoon grated cheese

½ teaspoon salt

1 pound ham, finely chopped

1 egg yolk

2 tablespoons sour cream

Rinse spinach well; cook, drain, chop fine and let cool. Melt butter; add flour to make a light roux and cool. Beat egg yolks well; add cheese, roux and spinach. Beat egg whites until stiff and add slowly to spinach mixture.

Grease and flour well a jelly roll pan. Pour in mixture and bake at 350 degrees for 20 minutes. To make filling, mix together finely chopped ham, egg yolk and sour cream. When spinach mixture is baked, turn out on a damp cloth; fill and roll up. Serve hot.

Mrs. Janja Loncar
Embassy of Yugoslavia

Spinach, Feta and Farmer's Cheese en Croute

SERVES 8 TO 10

2 packages (or 2 pounds) puff pastry dough, defrosted in refrigerator over night

1 package spinach, stems removed and sliced

6-ounce package farmer's cheese

½ pound feta cheese

Sesame seeds

Wesson oil

Preheat the oven to 425 degrees. Place spinach in a large bowl, add farmer's cheese crumbled with a fork. Cut in feta and mix.

Grease a 10x14-inch baking dish well. Roll out dough and drape it over the edge of the dish. Add spinach mixture and distribute evenly. Add another sheet of dough over the top and join edges. Brush top with Wesson oil and sprinkle with sesame seeds. Bake for 15 minutes. Turn down the temperature to 350 degrees and bake for another 5 minutes.

Miriam Benbassat

Cheese Soufflé

SERVES 6 TO 8

6 cup soufflé mold with collar

4 tablespoons butter (1 tablespoon reserved for buttering mold)

1 teaspoon Parmesan cheese, grated

3 tablespoons flour

1 cup boiling milk

½ teaspoon salt

⅛ teaspoon pepper

Pinch of cayenne pepper

Pinch of nutmeg

4 egg yolks

Scant teaspoon of cream of tartar

5 egg whites

Pinch of salt

¾ cup Swiss cheese, grated coarsely

Butter inside of soufflé mold and sprinkle with Parmesan cheese.

Melt 3 remaining tablespoons of butter in a saucepan. Stir in flour with a wooden spoon and cook over moderate heat until mixture foams together for 2 minutes. Do not allow it to brown. Remove from heat and when mixture has stopped bubbling, pour in all the boiling milk at once. Beat vigorously with a wire whisk until well blended. Beat in the seasonings. Return over moderately high heat and boil, stirring with the wire whisk for about a minute. Sauce will be thick.

Remove from heat. Separate the 4 eggs, putting the whites into one bowl and the yolks into the hot sauce. Beat the yolks one at a time into the sauce with a wire whisk. Correct seasoning. (The sauce may be prepared ahead to this point, dot the top of the sauce with butter. Heat to tepid before continuing.) Preheat oven to 400 degrees.

Beat 5 egg whites with the salt until stiff. Add a scant teaspoon of cream of tartar and beat again. Stir a large teaspoon of the egg whites into the sauce. Stir in all but a tablespoon of the cheese. Carefully fold in the rest of the egg whites.

Turn the soufflé mixture into the prepared mold which should be almost three quarters full. Tap bottom of the mold lightly on the table and smooth the surface of the soufflé with the flat of a knife. Sprinkle the remaining cheese on top.

Place in the middle of the preheated oven and immediately turn heat down to 375 degrees. Do not open oven door for 20 minutes. In 25 to 30 minutes, the soufflé will puff up about 2 inches above the rim of the mold and the top will be nicely browned. Bake 5 minute more to firm it up. Serve at once.

Cookbook Committee

Eggs on Tomatoes and Peppers for Brunch

SERVES 9

2 packages frozen, chopped green peppers

2 cloves garlic, sliced

6 cans stewed tomatoes, drained

1 8-ounce can tomato sauce

1 bunch parsley, chopped

9 eggs

1 tablespoon oil

Salt to taste

In a large skillet, sauté peppers in a small amount of oil. Remove from heat and add the sliced garlic. Add drained tomatoes, tomato sauce, parsley and salt to taste. Return to heat and simmer to reduce liquid. (At this point, you can refrigerate overnight in the baking dish.)

Preheat oven to 350 degrees. Bring tomato mixture to room temperature. Make indentations with the back of a spoon and break the eggs into the small craters. Bake in a 10x14-inch baking dish for one hour or until done, checking occasionally.

‾
Miriam Benbassat

Mushroom and Cheese Strata

SERVES 8 TO 10

3 tablespoons unsalted butter

1 small onion

10 ounces mushrooms

¼ cup parsley

¾ pound Gruyère cheese, coarsely shredded

6 large eggs

½ teaspoon salt

¼ teaspoon pepper

2 teaspoons Dijon mustard

1⅔ cups milk

⅔ cup light cream

9 slices challah (egg bread)

Melt butter. Stir in onion and cook for 2 minutes. Stir in mushrooms and parsley. Cook 2 to 3 minutes. Cool. Add salt and pepper. Butter bread and tear into pieces. Scatter half of bread on bottom of 9x12-inch baking dish. Top with half of cheese. Spoon the mushroom mixture evenly on top. Top with remaining cheese and bread.

Whisk egg, milk, cream, mustard and additional salt and pepper to taste. Pour over top. Cover with plastic wrap, and refrigerate for 6 to 8 hours or overnight.

Bake at 350 degrees for 50 to 60 minutes or until puffy, completely set and golden on top.

‾
Alice Kogan Weinreb
NSO Flute

Sausage and Egg Casserole

SERVES 10

1 package Regular Flavor Jimmy Dean's Sausage, may be cooked ahead

10 eggs, lightly beaten

3 cups milk (preferably 2%)

2 teaspoons dry mustard

6 cups cubed bread (can use Italian loaf, rye, whole grain, or a combination)

2 cups sharp cheddar cheese, shredded

½ teaspoon black pepper

1 teaspoon salt

Preheat oven to 325 degrees. Cook sausage and crumble until no longer pink. In a large mixing bowl combine eggs, milk, dry mustard and salt.

Butter a 9x13x2-inch baking dish. Distribute half of cubed bread into baking dish. Sprinkle half of pepper, cheese and sausage over bread. Repeat layering. Pour egg mixture over casserole. Bake uncovered for 60 minutes, until eggs set. Cover with foil if the top browns too quickly.

Katie Tardio
NSO Women's Committee Member

Breakfast Casserole

SERVES 6

¼ cup butter

6 slices bread

1 pound of breakfast sausage, cooked and sliced

5 eggs, beaten

2 cups milk

1 teaspoon dry mustard

1½ cups shredded cheddar cheese

Melt butter in a 9x13x2-inch glass casserole dish. Dice bread and place in casserole. Slice sausage over bread cubes.

In a separate bowl, beat eggs, milk and mustard. Sprinkle cheese over sausage layer and then top with egg mixture. Soak at least 30 minutes or overnight. Bake at 350 degrees, covered with foil, for 40 to 45 minutes.

Christina Rossetti

Prosciutto and Spinach Frittata

SERVES 4

3 large eggs

¼ cup heavy cream

½ cup Parmesan cheese, grated

4 slices prosciutto, julienned

Salt and pepper

¼ package frozen spinach, defrosted

2 tablespoons olive oil

Beat the eggs and add the cream, Parmesan cheese, and strips of prosciutto. Season with fresh pepper. Fold in the spinach and mix well. Set aside for 10 minutes.

Heat one tablespoon of olive oil in a 6-inch omelet pan. When hot, add the egg mixture. Cook 15 minutes over a low flame. Make sure the mixture does not stick to the pan. Now set the pan under the broiler just to form a crust. Do not leave it, or it will burn.

Turn frittata upside down into a dish. Wipe out the omelet pan, add the second tablespoon of olive oil and heat. When hot, replace frittata in the pan, bottom side up and cook once again on a low flame another 15 minutes.

When done, the frittata will be about one inch thick. Dry it on absorbent paper to eliminate all the oil. It can be served cold or warm, as an appetizer, snack or luncheon dish.

Cookbook Committee

Spinach Frittata

SERVES 4 TO 6

3 tablespoons olive oil

½ cup onion, thinly sliced

10 eggs

1 cup raw spinach (½ pound), finely chopped

⅓ cup Parmesan cheese, grated

1 tablespoon parsley, chopped

1 small clove garlic, crushed

Salt and pepper

Preheat oven to 350 degrees. Heat oil in a 10-inch heavy skillet with heat resistant handles. Add onions until golden, about 5 minutes.

In a large bowl, combine remaining ingredients and turn into skillet with the onion. Cook over low heat, lifting from bottom as eggs set, for about 3 minutes. Bake uncovered for 10 minutes, until the top sets. With a spatula loosen bottom and edges and slide onto a serving platter.

Katie Tardio
NSO Women's Committee Member

The National Symphony Orchestra performs at the Herod Atticus Theater, Athens, Greece (1976). Photo from NSO Archives.

Note: *recipes marked with this icon are from the original National Symphony Orchestra Cookbook, published by FANS (Friends Assisting the National Symphony) in 1983.*

SALADS

SALADS

California Salad with Lemon Dressing

SERVES 8 TO 10

This is my favorite summer salad, beautiful to behold and wonderful to eat.

1 head Boston lettuce

1 pint cherry tomatoes, halved

1 medium cantaloupe

2 11-ounce cans mandarin orange sections, drained

½ cup pitted black olives

2 avocados, peeled, sliced, sprinkled with lemon

1 sweet Italian onion, sliced very thin

3 heads Belgian endive, leaves separated

LEMON DRESSING

3 tablespoons fresh lemon juice

⅛ teaspoon salt

Freshly ground pepper to taste

¼ cup salad oil

¼ cup olive oil

1 teaspoon dried basil or 2 tablespoons fresh chopped basil

Chill lettuce, tomatoes, cantaloupe, orange sections, olives, avocados, onion and endives.

Using a large, wide salad bowl, line sides and bottom with lettuce leaves. Stand endive leaves straight up behind lettuce, like flower petals. Arrange chilled ingredients inside, using your artistic abilities.

To make dressings, combine lemon juice, salt, pepper, salad oil, olive oil and basil; mix well with a whisk or shake together in a bottle.

Drizzle dressing over salad after your guests have seen your work of art, and toss lightly until ingredients are well coated. Serve immediately.

Note: Leave avocado pit in avocado until you are ready to toss salad with dressing. The pit will keep avocado from turning dark.

Lonie Landfield

Salade Niçoise

SERVES 6

¾ pound red potatoes

1½ tablespoons Dijon mustard

5 cloves garlic (peeled, crushed and chopped)

1½ tablespoons red wine vinegar

7 tablespoons extra virgin olive oil

2 teaspoons salt

3 teaspoons freshly ground pepper

¾ pound string beans (tips snapped off, preferably haricots verts)

1 yellow pepper

2 ripe medium tomatoes

1 large red onion (sliced)

1 cup Niçoise olives

1 pound fresh tuna (cut into ½-inch cubes)

1 teaspoon olive oil

1 cup basil leaves (shredded)

Place the potatoes in a saucepan, cover with cool water and bring the water to a boil over high heat. Cover, reduce heat to low and gently boil for 25 minutes, until potatoes are tender but still firm when pierced with a fork. Drain off the water and set aside until cool enough to slice.

Prepare the dressing: In a large bowl, mix together the mustard, garlic, vinegar, olive oil, 1 teaspoon of salt and 1 teaspoon of pepper.

Peel the potatoes and cut into ½-inch slices. Toss with the dressing.

Bring the beans to a boil in a saucepan. Boil 3 to 4 minutes for haricots verts and up to 7 minutes for larger beans. Drain and run under cool water for a few seconds to stop the cooking and to preserve the color. Cut beans in half.

Clean yellow peppers; discard the seeds. Cut them into julienne strips. Cut tomatoes into small wedges; discard seeds.

Add the beans, yellow pepper, red onions, tomatoes and black olives to the potatoes. Mix well.

When almost ready to serve, heat a large skillet for 4 minutes until very hot. Sprinkle the tuna with salt, pepper and oil. Place tuna cubes in the skillet and sauté for 2 minutes.

To serve: Line platter with lettuce leaves. Mound Salade Niçoise in the center and add the freshly cooked tuna and basil leaves on top. Serve immediately.

Cookbook Committee

Fatoosh

SERVES 4 TO 6

2 loaves Arab or flat bread (stale or toasted bread is excellent)

1 small bunch fresh mint, minced

1 bunch of scallions, minced

Juice of 2 lemons

⅓ cup olive oil

1 head Romaine lettuce

1 large cucumber, peeled

1 small bunch parsley, minced

Salt and freshly ground pepper to taste

1 clove garlic (optional)

This is extra special when served cold on a hot summer day.

In a large bowl break bread into bite-size pieces. Cut vegetables into small pieces and add to bread.

Add other ingredients and mix well.

Embassy of Lebanon

Hearts of Palm Salad

SERVES 6

SALAD
2 heads of Bibb lettuce

2 14-ounce cans palm hearts, chilled

12 thin slices pimento

6 large sprigs parsley

DRESSING
1 shallot

½ cup garlic vinegar

1 tablespoon lemon juice

1 teaspoon dry mustard

1 whole egg

1 egg yolk

⅔ teaspoon anchovy paste

1½ cups virgin olive oil

The dressing, a great favorite, is also wonderful for a chef's salad.

Carefully separate Bibb lettuce leaves and wash well in cold water. Drain and spin dry and set aside. Drain palm hearts and refresh under cold water.

Arrange lettuce leaves on 6 chilled salad plates. Center palm hearts on beds of lettuce.

Pour dressing over salads and garnish with pimento slices and parsley springs.

DRESSING
Place shallot, garlic vinegar, lemon juice, dry mustard, egg, egg yolk and anchovy paste in an electric blender or food processor; blend well. Continue processing while adding olive oil in a thin stream until well blended.

Chef George Gianakos
The Prime Rib Restaurant

Spinach, Arugula and Carrot Salad

SERVES 8

8 ounces baby spinach

4 ounces arugula

1 carrot, finely sliced

6 green onions, minced

3 slices bacon

½ clove garlic

Sliced mushrooms

1 tablespoon olive oil

Balsamic vinegar

1 teaspoon sugar

Salt and pepper

Cut stems from spinach. Wash salad greens in cold water. Drain and blot dry. Tear leaves into bite-sized pieces.

Mince onions. Mix with greens in a wooden bowl. Add carrot to greens. Mash ½ clove garlic with 1 tablespoon of olive oil. Let stand 30 minutes. Discard garlic and trickle garlic oil over spinach; let stand. Add sliced mushrooms. Mix oil and balsamic vinegar. Add sugar, salt and pepper to taste.

Sauté 3 pieces of bacon until crisp, remove and drain on paper towel. Save any bacon fat; add a little bacon fat to dressing to thicken slightly. Pour over greens and toss well. Crumble bacon and sprinkle over salad.

Loren Kitt
NSO Principal Clarinet

Tabbouleh Salad

SERVES 8

2 cups cracked Bulgur wheat

1 pound black Kalamata olives, pitted

1 large clove garlic, crushed

1 pound tomatoes, seeded and chopped

2 cups green onions, chopped

3 cups parsley, chopped

¼ cup fresh mint, chopped

½ cup olive oil

½ cup or less fresh lemon juice

Salt and pepper to taste

4 cups boiling water

Rinse wheat and cover with the boiling water. Add garlic, cover, and let stand 30 minutes or until fluffy. Add to wheat the olives, tomatoes, onions, parsley and mint. Gently mix.

In a separate bowl, add lemon juice. Whisk in the olive oil. Pour over wheat mixture and gently mix. Season with salt and pepper to taste.

Cookbook Committee

Summer Salad

SERVES 8

2-3 heads Romaine lettuce, chopped

8 stalks celery, thinly sliced

6 green onions, thinly sliced and chopped

1 11-ounce can mandarin orange sections, drained

½-¾ pound bacon, cooked, cooled and crumbled

VINAIGRETTE DRESSING
½ cup vegetable oil

2 tablespoons sugar

4 tablespoons white vinegar

1 teaspoon salt to taste

½ teaspoon pepper to taste

12-15 drops hot sauce

CARMELIZED ALMONDS
¾ cup slivered almonds

5 tablespoons sugar

Great to prepare ahead of time! If you are traveling, take separate Ziploc bags with oranges, dressing, bacon and almonds. Add to salad just before serving and mix well.

CARAMELIZED ALMONDS

In a Teflon coated frying pan combine slivered almonds and sugar and cook over medium heat until the sugar melts completely and the almonds begin to brown. Stir often. When caramelized, pour onto release aluminum foil and immediately break into small pieces and store in air tight container.

SUMMER SALAD

Mix together Romaine lettuce, celery and green onions. If traveling, place each ingredient in a separate Ziploc bag. Then combine ingredients to make salad just before serving and mix well. Add mandarin orange sections, crumbled bacon and caramelized almonds to salad. Pour vinaigrette dressing over salad and toss well.

Crumbled bacon, caramelized almonds and the vinaigrette dressing can be made ahead of time.

Nancy Joan Crum
NSO Women's Committee Member

Pea Salad Vinaigrette

SERVES 8

This salad is colorful, tasty, easy and refreshingly different!

2 10-ounce packages frozen peas (tiny or regular size)

½ cup salad oil

3 tablespoons red wine vinegar

2 tablespoons scallions, finely chopped

1 tablespoon parsley, minced

1 tablespoon diced pimento

2 tablespoons sweet pickles, finely chopped

Freshly ground pepper to taste

1 teaspoon salt

Cook frozen peas by pouring boiling water over them to cover. Let stand for approximately 3 minutes and drain.

Combine salad oil, wine vinegar, scallions, pickles, parsley, pimento, salt and pepper in a jar. Cover and shake well to make dressing.

Pour dressing over peas and refrigerate at least 2 hours; make a day ahead if possible. Toss lightly before serving.

Marnie Nicholson
Former NSO FANS Member

Watercress, Endive and Orange Salad

SERVES 6 TO 8

3 endives

1 bunch watercress

2-3 oranges

MUSTARD DRESSING
½ cup vegetable oil

2 tablespoons olive oil

2 tablespoons cider vinegar

1 teaspoon honey

1 tablespoon Dijon mustard

2-3 peeled and chopped shallots

Wash endives and cut lengthwise into thin strips. Wash, dry and trim watercress. Peel and slice oranges.

On a large platter, arrange watercress in a circle. Place endive strips around watercress and put oranges in middle.

MUSTARD DRESSING
To make dressing, place all ingredients in a blender or food processor and blend well. Pour over salad.

Jane Lehrman
Former NSO FANS Member

Salat Olivier

2 large whole chicken breasts, halved

1 large onion, peeled and quartered

1 teaspoon salt

4 new potatoes, boiled, peeled and thinly sliced

3 hard-boiled eggs, peeled and thinly sliced

3 spring onions, chopped

½ cup celery, chopped

1 teaspoon salt

⅛ teaspoon white pepper

½ cup mayonnaise

1 cup sour cream

1 tablespoon fresh dill, minced

1 medium tomato, peeled and cut lengthwise into eighths

Lettuce leaves

In a heavy 2 to 3 quart pot, combine chicken, onion quarters and salt. Cover with about 1½ quarts cold water and bring to a boil, uncovered, over high heat, skimming off fat and scum as it rises to surface. Partially cover pan, reduce heat to low and simmer 15 to 20 minutes or until chicken is tender.

Chill cooked chicken breasts, if desired. With a sharp knife, remove and discard skin and cut meat away from bones. Cut meat into strips about ½ inch wide and combine them in a large mixing bowl with potatoes, eggs, celery and spring onions. Sprinkle with salt and white pepper.

In a small bowl, combine mayonnaise and sour cream and stir half of it into salad. Taste for seasoning.

To serve, place salad on lettuce leaves and garnish with sliced tomato. Top with dressing and sprinkle dill over all.

—
Cathy Tennyson
Former NSO FANS Member

Greek Salad

SERVES 4

1 seedless cucumber, chopped

½ green bell pepper, chopped

½ small red onion, sliced

⅓ cup Kalamata olives

1 cup cherry tomatoes, halved

1 5-ounce piece feta cheese, quartered

DRESSING

2 tablespoons extra virgin olive oil

2 teaspoons fresh lemon juice

Fresh black pepper

Toss all ingredients together. In a small bowl whisk the olive oil with the lemon juice. Mix into the salad.

Cookbook Committee

Warm Potato Salad

SERVES 4

2 pounds new potatoes, cleaned and cut into bite-size pieces

4-5 slices bacon

½ red pepper, cut into ½-inch cubes

3 green onions, sliced

1 clove garlic, minced

1 tablespoon white wine vinegar

1 tablespoon red wine vinegar

1½ tablespoons Dijon mustard

2 tablespoons fresh herbs, chopped (parsley, chives and/or rosemary)

Salt and freshly ground pepper

Place potatoes in a 2-quart pan and cover with cold water. Add 2 teaspoons salt, bring to a rapid boil, then decrease heat and continue cooking until tender. Drain well.

Meanwhile cook bacon, reserving ¼ cup of bacon fat in pan in which bacon was cooked. Crumble bacon and return to pan. Add red pepper, onions, garlic, vinegars, mustard, herbs, salt and pepper. Mix well.

Place potatoes in a heat-proof bowl, add bacon dressing and mix well. Correct seasonings. Keep warm in a 200 degree oven until ready to serve.

Cookbook Committee

Warm Chicken Salad

SERVES 8

4 cups cold, cut up chicken chunks (cooked)

2 tablespoons lemon juice

¾ cup mayonnaise

1 teaspoon salt

2 cups chopped celery

4 hard-boiled eggs, sliced

¾ cup cream of chicken soup

1 teaspoon finely minced onion

1 whole pimento, cut fine

1½ cups crushed potato chips

1 cup grated cheese

⅔ cup finely chopped, toasted almonds

Combine all ingredients except cheese, potato chips and almonds. Place in a large rectangular dish. Top with remaining 3 ingredients.

Let stand overnight in refrigerator. Bake in 400 degree oven for 20 to 25 minutes.

Mrs. Richard M. Nixon
Former First Lady

Spinach and Mushroom Salad

SERVES 6

10 ounces fresh spinach

6 slices lean bacon, broiled until crisp

1 bunch scallions, sliced

¼ pound mushrooms, sliced

2 tablespoons lemon juice

6 tablespoons olive oil

¾ teaspoon salt

⅛ teaspoon pepper, freshly ground

1 finely minced garlic clove

⅛ teaspoon dry mustard

¼ teaspoon sugar

1 egg yolk

Trim, thoroughly wash and dry spinach. Place in salad bowl.

Crumble bacon over spinach; add scallions and mushrooms. Chill.

Combine remaining ingredients and blend well. Chill. Use to dress salad.

Loren Kitt
NSO Principal Clarinet

Les Crudités Obernoises

SERVES 6 TO 8

2 teaspoons finely minced onion

1 tablespoon peanut oil

1 teaspoon white wine vinegar

½ teaspoon salt

Freshly ground white pepper

1 pound Gruyère cheese

6 large, fresh beets

Salt to taste

6 large carrots

4 medium-size celery roots

Fresh chopped parsley

REMOULADE SAUCE
1 cup mayonnaise

1½ teaspoons dry mustard

⅛ teaspoon sugar

½ teaspoon lemon juice

With pâté, French bread and wine, this is a meal in itself.

Combine onion, oil, salt and white pepper to form dressing. Set aside. Remove rind from Gruyère cheese and cut into julienne strips the size of matchsticks. Place in a bowl and gently toss with half dressing.

Cook beets in lightly salted, boiling water about 35 to 45 minutes or until done. Drain. When cool enough to handle, peel and slice into julienne strips. Place in a bowl and toss with remaining dressing. Peel carrots and grate on a medium-size grater. Place in a bowl and season lightly with salt. Peel celery roots, cut into julienne strips, and place in a bowl.

REMOULADE SAUCE
Combine all ingredients of Remoulade Sauce and mix gently with celery root until well coated.

Arrange Gruyère, beets, carrots and celery root on a large plate in separate, carefully formed piles. Garnish with generous portions of chopped parsley and serve.

Chef François Haeringer
L'Auberge Chez François

Macaroni Salad

SERVES 20

8 cups dry macaroni (cooked and drained)

3 large cans crushed pineapple, undrained

2 cans tuna in water, undrained

2 cups celery, diced

Worcestershire sauce to taste

Salt and pepper

Mayonnaise, as needed

Mix thoroughly all ingredients.

—

Cookbook Committee

Springtime Roast Beef Salad

SERVES 2

SALAD
¼ pound cooked roast beef, cut in julienne strips

14 asparagus stalks, peeled and cooked

4 medium mushroom caps, cut in julienne strips

3 tablespoons blue cheese, crumbled

3 scallions, minced

1 tablespoon parsley, chopped

1 tablespoon chives, chopped

6 leaves Romaine lettuce, washed, dried and left whole

DRESSING
1 teaspoon prepared mustard

2 tablespoons red wine vinegar

¼ cup olive oil

Salt and freshly ground pepper to taste

½ clove garlic, minced

Wonderful luncheon dish!

SALAD
Place 3 Romaine leaves on each of two salad plates. Place asparagus on plates as in spokes of a bike.

In a 1-quart mixing bowl, toss together mushrooms, roast beef, scallions and parsley. Place half roast beef mixture on center of each plate. Pour some dressing over roast beef. Sprinkle salad with blue cheese and chives. Pass remaining dressing on side.

DRESSING
Mix mustard, vinegar, salt, pepper and garlic well. Slowly add olive oil. Set aside.

Salad can be made several hours in advance, covered with plastic and stored in refrigerator. Bring to room temperature ½ hour before serving.

Julia M. Logue-Riordan

Black Bean and Feta Salad

SERVES 4 TO 6

2 15-ounce cans black beans, rinsed and drained

4-5 scallions, sliced very thin

1 4-ounce package crumbled feta cheese

2 tablespoons olive oil

1 teaspoon Cavender's Greek seasoning or more to taste

Combine all above ingredients in medium size bowl. Cover and chill overnight or for at least 6 hours before serving.

Janet Waln
NSO Women's Committee Member

Cold Black Bean Salad

SERVES 10 TO 12

1 bunch cilantro

3 tomatoes

½ medium sweet Vidalia onion

½ medium Bermuda onion

½ green bell pepper

½ red bell pepper

2 jalapeno peppers

2 1 pound 13-ounce cans of Goya black beans

3 ears of sweet yellow corn or 1 bag of frozen sweet corn

½ cup olive oil

½ cup balsamic vinegar

8 ounces salsa

Salt and pepper to taste

4 dashes Tabasco

Sour cream, optional

Shredded cheddar cheese, optional

Chop cilantro. Dice tomatoes, onions and peppers. Open cans of black beans and rinse. Boil fresh corn for 8 minutes or until tender. For frozen corn, boil 3 minutes. Cut kernels off of the cob.

Combine cilantro, diced tomatoes, onions, peppers, black beans and corn into a large mixing bowl. Add olive oil, balsamic vinegar, salsa, salt, pepper and Tabasco to bowl. Mix thoroughly until evenly blended. Amounts of spices, oil and vinegar can be modified to your taste preferences.

To serve hot, add 1 cup of water and then simmer all of the ingredients except beans and vinegar for 30 minutes. The hot version omits the vinegar. Add the beans after 30 minutes and simmer for an additional 10 minutes. The total cooking time is 40 minutes.

Top the hot black bean salad with sour cream and cheese.

Jovita M. Gross
Kennedy Center Administrative Staff Member

Broccoli Cauliflower Salad

SERVES 10 TO 12

3 cups broccoli florets

3 cups cauliflower florets

1 large carrot, shredded

¼ cup finely chopped red onion or 2 green onions, chopped

1 cup mayonnaise

2 tablespoons vinegar

2 tablespoons sugar

½ cup pecans, halves or pieces, toasted

½ cup dried cherries

Stir the dry vegetables to mix. Combine mayonnaise, vinegar and sugar in a small bowl. Add mayonnaise mixture to vegetables and mix well, coating all of the vegetables. Chill for two hours or overnight. Garnish with cherries and nuts, optional.

Ms. Jannie L. Roher
NSO Women's Committee Member

Potato Salad

SERVES 6

¼ cup Italian dressing

5 medium potatoes

1 cup celery, chopped

1 onion, chopped

4 hard-boiled eggs, sliced

1½ teaspoons salt

½ cup mayonnaise (Duke's if available)

Wash and then boil the potatoes for 15 to 20 minutes, until soft. Remove from water and allow to cool. Peel and cube potatoes. Pour Italian dressing over the still warm potatoes and then chill for 2 hours.

Add chopped celery, chopped onion, sliced eggs and salt to chilled potatoes. Add mayonnaise and mix carefully. Chill for at least 4 hours. If you can, allow the salad to chill for a day.

Jennifer Carrier
NSO Administrative Staff Member

Peas and Green Bean Salad

SERVES 8 TO 10

1 cup vinegar

½ cup vegetable oil

1 cup sugar

1 can very small peas (1 lb. 1 oz.), drained

1 14½-ounce can French style green beans, drained

1 cup celery, chopped

1 onion, finely chopped

1 4-ounce jar pimentos

Dissolve sugar in vinegar and oil. Add other ingredients and mix thoroughly. Refrigerate 24 hours. Drain before serving. This keeps well for several days if refrigerated.

Doris A. Criswell
NSO Women's Committee Member

The National Symphony Orchestra in Constitution Hall with Founding Music Director, Hans Kindler (1931). Photo from NSO archives.

BREADS

BREADS

Mrs. Lyndon B. Johnson's Popovers

MAKES 6 TO 8 POPOVERS

"This is one of our favorite 'house dishes.' Our friends know they're sure to have popovers for one meal during a house party."

1 cup sifted flour

1 cup milk

2 eggs, beaten

¼ teaspoon salt

2 tablespoons shortening, melted

Mix and sift flour and salt. Combine eggs, milk and shortening. Add gradually to flour mixture, beating about 1 minute or until batter is smooth.

Fill greased, sizzling-hot pans three-quarters full and bake in very hot oven (450 degrees) for about 20 minutes. Reduce heat to 350 degrees and continue baking for 15 to 20 minutes.

Lady Bird Johnson
Former First Lady

Quick Icebox Rolls

MAKES 18 TO 24 ROLLS

¾ cup milk

¼ cup sugar

3 tablespoons shortening

1 teaspoon salt

1 package yeast

¼ cup lukewarm water

1 egg, beaten

3½ cups flour

Butter

Scald milk. Add sugar, shortening, salt and cool to lukewarm. Soften yeast in warm water. Add yeast and beaten egg to milk mixture. Add flour, ½ cup at a time, and knead.

Put dough in a greased bowl and grease top half of dough. Place in refrigerator. When ready to bake, take dough out of refrigerator, roll on floured board to about ½ inch thickness and cut out circles with biscuit cutter. Place small chunk of butter in middle of circle and fold over. Let rise until double in bulk. Bake at 425 degrees for 20 minutes.

Loren Kitt
NSO Principal Clarinet

Sweet Rolls

Makes 3 dozen

2 packages yeast

2 cups very warm water

½ cup sugar

2 teaspoons salt

¼ cup butter, softened

1 egg, beaten

6½-7 cups flour

Brown Sugar

Dissolve the yeast in water in electric mixer bowl. Stir in everything except the flour. Use the dough hook to stir in the flour a cup at a time. Knead until smooth and forms a large ball (no longer clings to the bowl).

Place dough in a buttered bowl. Turn it over so that the top of the dough is nicely buttered. Cover with plastic wrap and place a plate on top. Place in the refrigerator until you are ready to shape the rolls, but refrigerate for at least one night. It will be fine for 4 to 5 days.

To Shape the Rolls

Start about 2 hours before you want to bake them. Divide the dough (on a well-floured board) into 3 or 4 portions. Roll out each portion into a rectangle and spread with butter, and then with soft brown sugar. Roll up (like a jelly roll) and cut into slices about 1½ inches thick. Place each slice in a muffin tin cup that has been well buttered and has a nice "blob" of brown sugar in the bottom.

Cover the muffin tins with dish towels and place in a warm, draft-free place to rise. It might take an hour. When rolls are nice and plump looking, they are ready to bake in a 375 or 400 degree oven. Watch them closely; sometimes it only takes 10 minutes per batch.

Turn the pan upside down on sheets of foil while still warm and the sugar in the bottom will drip out of the tins.

To freeze, cool rolls (do not turn them upside down until you thaw them later) and wrap well.

Sally Gerber Phinny
NSO National Trustee

Bohemian Rye Bread

MAKES 2 LOAVES

2 packages dry yeast

2 cups warm water

¼ cup brown sugar or molasses

3 cups all-purpose flour

2 cups rye flour

2 teaspoons salt

3 tablespoons melted shortening

1 tablespoon caraway seeds

1 teaspoon cornstarch

½ cup water

Combine warm water and brown sugar or molasses. Sprinkle in dry yeast. Stir in 1 cup of each of the flours. Beat until smooth. Let stand 20 minutes or until spongy.

Stir in cooled, melted shortening, salt and caraway seeds. Add remaining flour to make soft dough. Knead on floured board until smooth and elastic, about 10 minutes, adding flour if necessary.

Let rise in covered, greased bowl in warm place until double in bulk. Punch down, knead several times, and allow to rest 20 to 30 minutes. Divide into 2 pieces and knead each into a smooth, round shape. Place in pie tins sprinkled with rye flour. Let bread rise until double in bulk.

Preheat oven to 375 degrees. Place pan of water in bottom of oven. Carefully spray loaves with water and bake about 40 to 50 minutes, spraying occasionally.

Mix cornstarch in water, boil and cook for 1 minute. Brush on baked loaves. Return loaves to oven for about 3 minutes.

C. Z. Serpan

Simply Simple Supper Bread

MAKES 4 LOAVES

This bread can be started from scratch 3 hours before dinner. It produces an Italian type loaf that goes well with almost any meal. If you make more than you need, put the remaining loaves in the freezer.

3 packages yeast

1 cup warm water

2 teaspoons sugar

3 cups warm water

½ cup oil (olive or corn)

2 teaspoons salt

6 cups white flour (approximately)

6 cups wheat flour (approximately)

Sesame seeds

Proof yeast by sprinkling yeast over 1 cup water, add sugar and let yeast dissolve. After about 5 minutes, it should start foaming.

Mix yeast, 3 cups water, oil and salt in a large bowl. Add flour alternating white and wheat. Mix as you add. When the dough is firm enough to knead, take it out of bowl and knead using additional white flour if necessary to keep from sticking. Knead for about 10 minutes.

Place dough in a buttered bowl and butter it all over. Cover and let rise for about 2 hours.

Divide dough into 4 parts. Shape into French style loaves. Place on oiled cookie sheets. Wet tops and sprinkle sesame seeds on top. Slash tops diagonally and place loaves in oven.

Turn oven to 400 degrees. Bake for 35 minutes or until done. Test by tapping bottom of loaf. If it sounds hollow, bread is done.

George Ziener
Former NSO FANS Member

Danish Buttermilk Bread

MAKES 2 LOAVES

2 cups buttermilk, scalded

4 tablespoons butter

1 tablespoon sugar

1 tablespoon salt

1 tablespoon yeast

¼ cup warm water

6 cups all-purpose flour, approximately

Melt butter in warm buttermilk. Cool. Soften yeast in warm water.

Add cooled buttermilk mixture to softened yeast. Add sugar and salt. Gradually mix in flour. Knead for 5 to 10 minutes. The dough should be soft but not sticky. Place in a bowl and let rise until double in bulk (approximately 1½ hours). Punch dough down. Repeat process if time permits.

Form into 2 loaves and place in 5x9-inch bread pans. Let rise until double in bulk (approximately 1½ hours).

Bake at 375 degrees for 35 minutes. Remove from pans and cool on rack. For extra touch, brush tops of warm loaves with butter.

VARIATIONS

For up to 2 cups of the white flour, substitute equal quantities of whole wheat flour, wheat germ, oatmeal, etc.

For cinnamon bread, before forming into loaves, roll each half of dough into a 9-inch wide rectangle. Rub surface of dough with soft butter and sprinkle with cinnamon, ground cloves or nutmeg and raisins and nuts. Roll up, beginning with 9-inch edge. Pinch edges together to seal. Place in bread pan, sealed edge down.

Ann Leonard

Danish Rye Bread

MAKES 1 LOAF

SPONGE
1 cup rye flour

½ cup buttermilk

½ teaspoon salt

BREAD
2 cups water

1 tablespoon salt

3 packages dry yeast

3-4 cups rye flour

SPONGE

Mix rye flour with buttermilk and salt. Cover with plastic wrap and keep in cool place for at least 2 days but not longer than 3 days.

BREAD

Stir sponge with water and salt. Add yeast. Add rye flour gradually until dough holds together. Dough will feel somewhat greasy. Knead for 8 to 10 minutes.

Let rise for 1 hour, shape dough into loaf and let rise again for 45 minutes. Dough will not double as wheat flour dough does. Punch bread with fork. Brush with water and melted butter.

Bake at 425 degrees in lower portion of oven for 1¼ to 1½ hours.

Susanne Misner

Granola Bread

MAKES 2 OR 3 LOAVES

2 packages dry yeast

2 teaspoons sugar

1 cup warm water

⅓ cup butter

1 cup boiling water

1 cup plain granola

½ cup dark molasses

1 tablespoon salt

5½ cups flour

1 egg

Mix yeast and sugar in 1 cup warm water and let stand 10 minutes.

Mix butter and boiling water until butter is melted. Combine granola, molasses and salt with butter and boiling water. Add yeast mixture and stir. Add egg. Stir in flour. Mix until sticky.

Refrigerate overnight or at least 2 to 4 hours.

Knead well. Shape into 2 or 3 loaves. Let rise until double in bulk. Bake in 350 degree oven for 1 hour for 2 loaves or 45 minutes for 3 loaves.

Ruth Thompson

Easy Oatmeal Bread

MAKES 2 LOAVES

2 cups boiling water

1 cup quick oats

½ cup whole wheat flour

3 tablespoons butter

1 teaspoon salt

½ cup brown sugar

2 packages dry yeast

½ cup warm water

5 cups all-purpose flour

Pour two cups boiling water over first 5 ingredients. Dissolve yeast in ½ cup warm water. Cool wheat flour mixture; then add yeast. Mix together. Add white flour until mixture gathers into a ball (you may not need all 5 cups). Knead on a floured board until smooth.

Put in greased bowl. Let rise until double in bulk (1½ to 2 hours). Punch down. Let rise again until double. Punch down.

Shape into 2 loaves. Let rise about 15 minutes. Bake at 350 degrees for 30 minutes.

Wynne B. Beaman

Alice's Fluffy Biscuits

NUMBER OF BISCUITS WILL DEPEND ON THE SIZE OF THE CUTTER

2 cups flour, sifted

4 teaspoons baking powder

1 teaspoon salt

2 teaspoons sugar

½ teaspoon cream of tartar

½ cup shortening

⅔ cup milk

Mix dry ingredients. Cut in shortening with 2 knives. Add milk and mix well.

Knead dough lightly; roll to desired thickness. Bake in 400 degree oven until brown.

Patrick Hayes
Former NSO General Manager

Bran Muffins

MAKES 2 TO 3 DOZEN

1 cup boiling water

1 cup 100% Bran cereal

1 cup sugar

¼ cup butter

¼ cup oil or shortening

2 eggs

1 cup flour

1½ cups whole wheat flour

2½ teaspoons baking soda

½ teaspoon salt

1¾ cups buttermilk

2 cups All-Bran cereal

¾ cup sunflower seeds

⅓ cup wheat germ

⅓ cup chopped dates

Mix all ingredients and refrigerate overnight. Do not stir again. Pour batter into muffin tins and bake at 400 degrees for 20 minutes.

VARIATION
Sunflower seeds, wheat germ and dates are optional.

Batter will keep in refrigerator for a few days.

Susan Koehler

Coffee Cake

SERVES 8 TO 12

½ pound butter

1 cup sugar

2 eggs

2 cups flour

1 teaspoon baking powder

1 teaspoon baking soda

1 cup sour cream

¼ teaspoon salt

1 teaspoon vanilla

½ cup sugar

1 tablespoon cinnamon

½ cup chopped nuts

Mix together sugar, cinnamon and nuts. Set aside. Mix together baking soda and sour cream. Set aside.

Cream butter with sugar. Add eggs and mix well. Add all dry ingredients and mix well. Add vanilla and sour cream mixture.

Spoon half of batter into greased tube or bundt pan and sprinkle with one-third of cinnamon-nut mixture. Add remainder of batter and sprinkle with cinnamon-nut mixture. Swirl with knife to marbelize. Sprinkle remaining cinnamon-nut mixture on top. Bake at 350 degrees for 35 to 45 minutes.

Cookbook Committee

Ruth Tozar's Favorite Coffee Cake

SERVES 8 TO 12

2½ cups flour

¾ cup white sugar

1 cup brown sugar

1 teaspoon nutmeg

½ teaspoon salt

¾ cup salad oil

1 cup sour milk

1 teaspoon baking soda

1 beaten egg

½ cup nuts

2 teaspoons cinnamon

Mix flour, brown and white sugar, nutmeg, salt and oil well. Remove ¾ cup of mixture and to it add nuts and cinnamon.

To rest of mixture add sour milk with baking soda and beaten egg. Mix well and put in a greased 8½x11-inch pan. Sprinkle nuts and cinnamon mixture on top.

Bake at 350 degrees for 1 hour.

Ruth Strickland Tozar

Katie's Coffee Cake

SERVES 9 TO 12

¼ pound butter, softened

1½ cups sugar

2 eggs

1 cup sour cream

2 teaspoons vanilla

2 cups flour, sifted

1 teaspoon baking powder

¼ teaspoon salt

⅓ cup chopped pecans

1 teaspoon cinnamon

Preheat oven to 325 degrees. Beat butter and 1 cup of sugar until fluffy. Beat in eggs one at a time. Stir in sour cream and vanilla. Add flour, baking powder, baking soda and salt. Stir into batter until smooth.

Spoon half of batter into greased 9-inch square baking pan. Combine remaining ½ cup sugar, nuts and cinnamon; sprinkle ⅔ of it over batter. Top remaining batter with remaining nut mixture. Bake for 50 minutes at 325 degrees or until done.

Katie Tardio
NSO Women's Committee Member

Lemon Bread

MAKES 2 LOAVES

1 cup butter

1¾ cups sugar

2 teaspoons baking powder

½ teaspoon salt

4 eggs, slightly beaten

2½ cups flour

1 cup milk

¾ cup coarsely chopped walnuts

Peel of 2 lemons, grated

Juice of 2 lemons

⅓-½ cup sugar

Cream sugar and butter together; combine baking powder, salt and eggs. Stir in flour and milk, alternating ingredients. Add nuts and lemon rind.

Pour batter into 2 very well greased and floured loaf pans. Bake at 350 degrees for 1 hour or until done.

While bread is baking, mix sugar with lemon juice. When bread is done, remove from oven and pierce tops with a toothpick, making small holes. Pour lemon-sugar mixture over hot loaves.

Cool loaves on a wire rack.

Patty Perkins Andringa
NSO Board Member

Challah

MAKES ONE LOAF

1⅛ cups water

4 cups bread flour

¼ cup sugar

1 tablespoon coarse (kosher) salt

2 large eggs

3 tablespoons olive oil or canola oil

2 teaspoons yeast

This recipe utilizes an automatic bread machine. Follow instructions for the bread machine. Add ingredients to the baking pan in the order listed above. After you have added the oil, make a depression in a dry area of the flour and sprinkle the yeast there. Make sure the yeast does not touch any liquid.

For loaf-shaped challah, use the bread machine's full cycle.

For braided challah, select the bread machine's "dough" cycle and remove the challah from the bread machine after it has risen. Form the dough into three cylinders and braid them into a loaf. Brush top with egg yolk mixed with 1 teaspoon water. Bake in oven for 45 minutes at 350 degrees.

Alice Kogan Weinreb
NSO Flute

Cornell Bread

3 cups warm water (95 degrees to 100 degrees)

2 packages dry yeast

2 tablespoons honey

7-8 cups unbleached flour

⅓ cup full fat soy flour

½ cup skim milk powder

4 teaspoons salt

2 tablespoons vegetable oil

¼ cup wheat germ

"This bread was originated at Cornell University to produce a nutritionally improved bread so far superior to the commercial product that life could be sustained on bread and butter alone."

Put water, yeast and honey in bowl of electric mixer and let stand for 5 minutes while yeast dissolves. Sift flour, wheat germ, soy flour and milk powder together in a separate bowl. Begin stirring yeast mixture in electric mixer. Add salt and 3 cups of flour mixture. Beat for 2 minutes. Add oil and 3 more cups of flour mixture. Blend well and knead, either on floured board or using a dough hook, until smooth and elastic.

Turn dough into a greased bowl, brush top with soft butter, cover and let rise until double in bulk, about 1½ hours. Punch down, fold edges over and let rise another 20 minutes. Turn dough onto board and shape into 2 loaves. Place in greased or buttered loaf pans. Cover and let rise until doubled.

Bake loaves at 350 degrees for 50 to 60 minutes.

If in doubt, tap loaves with your finger after 50 minutes. If they sound hollow, they are done.

Frances Fogel

The National Symphony Orchestra with Music Director Howard Mitchell
(1954). Credit Hank Walker, Time Life Magazine.

Note: *recipes marked with this icon are from the original National Symphony Orchestra*
Cookbook, published by FANS (Friends Assisting the National Symphony) in 1983.

SEAFOOD

SEAFOOD

Tuna and Spinach "Sausage"

SERVES 4

1½ pounds fresh spinach (or 3 boxes frozen spinach), cooked and drained

7-ounce can of white tuna in oil

6 flat anchovy filets

2 slices of good bread

½ cup half and half

1 lemon

Cheesecloth

2 jumbo eggs

3 tablespoons dry bread crumbs

¼ cup pignoli

Freshly ground black pepper

⅓ cup olive oil

1 tablespoon lemon juice

Put cooked, drained spinach and all other ingredients except olive oil, lemon juice and lemon into food processor; chop coarsely. Shape resulting green mixture into a sausage-shaped form about 12 inches long. Wrap loaf in several layers of cheesecloth and tie both ends securely.

Place loaf in a close-fitting pan and simmer for 35 minutes. Allow to cool for 5 minutes and then remove cheesecloth. Let cool completely.

Cut loaf into ⅜-inch slices. Arrange them slightly overlapping on a platter. Sprinkle with olive oil and lemon juice and serve at room temperature; garnish with paper-thin lemon slices.

John L. Hurley, Jr.

Grilled Tuna

SERVES 6

⅓ cup oil

2 teaspoons red wine vinegar

1 teaspoon garlic powder

1 teaspoon garlic salt

6 4-ounce tuna steaks, ½ inch thick

1 tablespoon butter

½ pound mushrooms, sliced

2 ounces currants

½ teaspoon garlic powder

⅛ teaspoon white pepper

1 teaspoon fresh parsley

½ teaspoon salt or to taste

1 thin slice lemon per serving

1 sprig parsley per serving

Combine first 4 ingredients. Place tuna in dish in one layer and cover with oil mixture. Marinate several hours or overnight.

Heat butter until sizzling. Sauté mushrooms, currants and remaining seasonings for 30 seconds, stirring to combine. Remove immediately.

Grill tuna over charcoal 30 to 60 seconds per side until just opaque. Spoon 1½ ounces mushroom mixture across center. Garnish with lemon slice and parsley sprig.

This can also be served as an appetizer or first course.

The Pleasant Peasant Restaurant

Bistro Français Tuna

SERVES 6 TO 8

2 pounds fresh tuna, diced in 1-inch pieces

2 tablespoons olive oil

3 shallots, chopped

2 apples, sliced

3 tablespoons apple cider vinegar

1 pint heavy cream

Paprika, salt and pepper to taste

Sauté tuna in olive oil with the shallots. Remove tuna. In same frying pan, sauté sliced apples until tender. Remove apples, deglaze the pan with vinegar and add cream. Reduce sauce. Now add the tuna and simmer all for five minutes.

Gérard Cabrol
Bistro Français

Paupiette of Lemon Sole with Crabmeat and Coriander Sauce

SERVES 2 TO 3

3 3-ounce lemon sole filets

½ pound crabmeat

½ pound butter

¼ cup white wine

2 dashes Worcestershire sauce

Lemon juice from 2 lemons

Salt and freshly ground pepper to taste

Water

½ bunch coriander

Roll crabmeat in each 3-ounce filet of sole. Season as desired with salt and pepper and lemon juice. Sprinkle on rolled filets a dash of paprika for color and a little melted butter.

Broil 5 minutes; bake another 10 minutes in a 400 degree oven. Add water to bottom of pan as needed to keep fish from burning.

To make sauce, use pan that was used to cook filets. Add lemon juice, Worcestershire sauce, white wine and butter. After butter is melted, add coriander to sauce and mix together. Pour sauce over paupiettes of lemon sole.

Chef Ki Choi
Wintergarden Restaurant at The Watergate

Dilled Monkfish

SERVES 4

Monkfish is a relatively new but tasty fish in town. It can be tough if not cooked long enough.

4 monkfish filets (approximately 2 pounds)

½ cup melted butter

2 tablespoons lemon juice

2 tablespoons white wine

Chopped fresh dill

Dash of Tabasco

Put two gashes in each filet. Mix a sauce using butter, lemon juice, white wine, chopped dill and Tabasco. Pour sauce over filets, and broil for 10 to 20 minutes, turning once.

Mrs. A. A. Sommer
Former NSO FANS Member

Baked Stuffed Red Snapper

SERVES 4 TO 6

3-3½ pounds whole red snapper, cleaned

¼ pound each of coarsely chopped filet of haddock, shelled, raw shrimp, cooked ham and artichoke hearts

1 hard-boiled egg, finely chopped

1 medium onion, chopped

1 medium green pepper, chopped

3 cloves garlic, minced

4 tablespoons highest quality olive oil

2 tablespoons lemon juice

2 whole lemons

½ cup dry white wine

2 tablespoons butter

2 tablespoons flour

4 tablespoons minced fresh parsley

Pimento slices

Salt

Ground white pepper

Preheat oven to 400 degrees. Rub white pepper and salt into cavity of fish. Place in lightly oiled baking pan.

Sauté onion, garlic and green pepper in 2 tablespoons olive oil until onion is transparent but not brown. Add haddock, shrimp, ham and artichokes. Cook over medium heat while stirring for 3 to 4 minutes. Add 3 tablespoons wine and cook 3 or 4 minutes until shrimp is done. Add hard-boiled egg.

Stuff fish with mixture. Brush fins with 2 tablespoons each of lemon juice, white wine and olive oil. Reduce oven to 325 degrees. Bake in middle of oven for about 40 minutes or until fish flakes when pierced with fork. Transfer fish carefully to platter and keep warm.

SAUCE
Strain juices and add remaining white wine. Boil until reduced to about ¾ cup. Add butter and flour and whisk until smooth. Simmer until sauce begins to thicken. Remove from heat and add 4 tablespoons minced fresh parsley. Cut strips of pimento (about ½ inch slices) and place vertically across fish. Form a row of thin lemon slices from tail to gills. Pour sauce over entire fish and serve on a bed of parsley.

Adel Sanchez
NSO Assistant Principal Trumpet

Grenadin de Saumon Roti

SERVES 6

2½ pounds boned and skinned salmon filet

10 tablespoons butter

5 garlic cloves

¼ pound fresh girolles (wood mushrooms) or dried Polish mushrooms, soaked in warm water for 15 minutes *(available in gourmet sections of most food stores)*

7 ounces pearl onions

Chicken stock

Sugar

1 tomato

1 tablespoon fresh thyme

1 tablespoon fresh chives

Clarified butter

Cut 2½ pounds of boned and skinned salmon filet into 4 lengthwise strips. Trim off sharp edges and cut each strip into 1½-inch lengths to form oval shapes.

Sauté in 3 tablespoons of butter in a preheated pan ¼ pound fresh girolles (wood mushrooms) and 2 unpeeled, smashed garlic cloves. Season to taste with salt and pepper. Cook approximately 1½ minutes. Discard garlic and set aside.

Cook pearl onions in chicken stock. Remove from stock while still crisp and sauté in 1 tablespoons of butter with a pinch of sugar until light brown in color. Set aside.

Finely dice one peeled and seeded tomato. Mince 1 tablespoon each fresh thyme and chives. Set aside.

Heat pan with clarified butter. Cook grenadins of salmon 3 minutes per side over medium flame. Remove and arrange on each plate. Spoon around salmon 1 tablespoon girolles interspersed with 4 or 5 of pearl onions.

Melt 6 tablespoons of butter over low heat. Add 3 cloves smashed garlic, diced tomatoes and herbs; bring to a boil. Discard garlic and drizzle over each salmon arrangement.

Chef Yannick Cam
Le Pavillon Restaurant

Yellowtail Snapper or Rockfish Meunière

SERVES 2

2 yellowtail snapper filets (8 ounces) or 2 rockfish filets (8 ounces)

Flour

3 tablespoons butter

1 pound fresh mushrooms, sliced

1 tablespoon parsley, chopped

2 tablespoons dry sherry

3 tablespoons white port

1 tablespoon Maggi brand seasoning

2 teaspoons lemon butter (fresh lemon juice and butter mixed)

Salt and freshly ground pepper

Flour fish filets on both sides. Sauté in butter over medium heat until browned.

Add sliced mushrooms, parsley, sherry and port. The addition of wines should ignite fish. Let filets flambé until flame dies out.

Add Maggi seasoning, salt, pepper and lemon butter; put in a hot (450 degree) oven for 10 to 15 minutes. Serve at once.

Chef Kimsan Seng
Richard's Pier 20 Restaurant

Pecan Encrusted Salmon

SERVES 4

4 salmon filets

1½ tablespoons Dijon mustard

2 tablespoons melted butter

2 tablespoons honey

1 cup bread crumbs

¼ cup finely chopped pecans

1 tablespoon chopped fresh parsley

Salt and pepper to taste

Preheat oven to 350 degrees. Sprinkle salmon with salt and pepper. Combine Dijon mustard, butter and honey and brush on both sides of salmon. Combine bread crumbs and pecans and dip fish to coat well.

Place in a greased 13x9-inch baking dish and spoon extra bread crumbs and pecan mixture on top. Sprinkle chopped fresh parsley on top. Bake at 350 degrees for 15 to 20 minutes depending upon thickness of salmon.

Anna Pfeiffer
NSO Board Member

Oven-Baked Smelts

SERVES 8 AS AN APPETIZER

SERVES 4 AS A MAIN DISH

2 pounds smelts, head and tail removed, fish cleaned of all bones

4 ounces canned anchovies

2 cups heavy cream

2 teaspoons salt

½ teaspoon ground white pepper

2 tablespoons butter

Fresh dill for garnishing

Rinse fish and remove backbones. Sprinkle fish inside and out with salt and pepper. Lay fish in a shallow, buttered, oven-proof dish.

Mash anchovies into a paste and mix it with cream. Pour cream mixture over fish. Place in preheated 400 degree oven for 10 to 15 minutes. Do not cover.

Serve immediately from baking dish.

This dish is delicious served with steamed new potatoes seasoned with dill, boiled brussel sprouts and small tomatoes.

Mrs. Jaakko O. Iloniemi
Embassy of Finland

Lotte en Papillot

SERVES 4

4 fillets of lotte (lotte is a firm, white fish - can be replaced by a similar kind)

2 pounds asparagus

1 pound young potatoes

1 lemon

4 sprigs of dill

1 teaspoon salt

Pepper from mill

4 baking foils, 13x17 inches

Crème fraîche

Preheat oven to 350 degrees. Cook asparagus for 4 minutes in salt water. Take out and cook potatoes in the same water for 12 minutes. Cook some lemon peel in the water for 12 minutes. Cut asparagus in small pieces. Cut fish in quarters.

Spread a little butter in the four baking foils. Put mixture of potatoes and asparagus in the middle of the foil. Spread with dill; put the fish pieces on top. Take the four ends to the middle and bind them with a kitchen thread. Put the baking foils in the preheated oven and bake for 30 minutes. Serve mixture of crème fraîche, lemon juice and dill as an accompaniment.

Ilse von Alpenheim Doráti
Guest Artist, Pianist and Wife of Former NSO Music Director Antal Doráti, 1970-1977

Soufflé de Poisson à la Florentine with Sauce Mousseline

SERVES 6

½ pound skinless flounder, or sole filets

½ cup dry white wine

½ teaspoon salt

Freshly ground pepper to taste

2 tablespoons minced shallots or spring onions

3 cups cooked chopped spinach

3 tablespoons butter

3 tablespoons flour

1 cup boiling milk

Pinch nutmeg

1 egg yolk

5 egg whites

½ cup grated Swiss cheese

SAUCE MOUSSELINE

3 egg yolks

½ cup whipping cream

¼ cup fish liquor

6 ounces butter

Salt and freshly ground white pepper to taste

Lemon juice to taste

Cut filets into 6 parts. Roll up fish filets and fasten with a toothpick. Poach fish 8 to 10 minutes in wine, ½ teaspoon salt, pepper and shallots. Gently lift out fish and set aside. Boil down liquid to ¼ cup. Strain and reserve for sauce.

Cook spinach. Chop and "dry" by evaporating in a skillet over medium heat. Spread in bottom of buttered, oval, fireproof dish about 16 inches long.

Cook butter and flour about 3 minutes, but do not brown. Remove from heat, beat in boiling milk a little at a time and add remaining seasonings. Return to heat and boil, stirring 1 to 2 minutes. Off heat, beat in egg yolk. Cool to luke warm.

Beat egg whites and salt until stiff. Stir one quarter of them into soufflé base, then stir in ¼ cup cheese; fold, carefully, balance of egg whites into base.

Place rolled fish filets on spinach. Mound soufflé mixture over fish. Sprinkle remaining cheese over top. Bake 15 to 18 minutes in a preheated 425 degree oven or until soufflé has puffed and browned. Serve with mousseline on the side.

SAUCE MOUSSELINE
Beat egg yolks, cream and fish liquor over low heat until mixture gradually thickens into a light cream to coat a spoon.

Remove from heat; beat in butter, one tablespoon at a time until sauce thickens like hollandaise. Add seasonings as necessary.

Albert J. Beveridge, III
Former NSO Board Member

Psari-Plaki Baked Fish

Serves 6 to 8

"One cannot travel to the Greek Islands without being aware of the marvelous scent of the sea. This recipe is synonymous with Greece. With a little Ouzo it will take your imagination to the Greek fishing villages."

1 striped bass, 3-4 pounds (bream or haddock can be substituted)

4 small onions, chopped fine

1 clove garlic, chopped fine

Chopped fresh parsley

½ cup tomato juice, from fresh, ripe tomatoes, if possible

½ cup dry white wine

Salt and freshly ground pepper

Thick slices of fresh tomatoes (or drained, canned tomatoes)

½ cup olive oil (or salad oil)

Lemon juice

Clean, wash, drain and salt fish. Slice into steaks and put aside. Mix onions, garlic, 4 tablespoons parsley, tomato juice, wine, salt and pepper.

Grease a roasting pan with oil and lay a thick bed of chopped parsley over bottom.

Arrange slices of fish in pan and spread some of onion mixture over them. Top each with a slice of tomato and pour oil over all. Sprinkle generously with lemon juice and bake in a moderate oven (350 degrees) for about 1 hour. Serve garnished with sprigs of fresh parsley.

Andreas Makris
Former NSO Violin and Composer-in-Residence

Monkfish in a Crust of Garlic and Baby Carrots

SERVES 4

1 potato

4 cloves of garlic

¼ pound heavy cream

½ teaspoon salt

2 teaspoons water

2 leeks

16 baby carrots

2 tablespoons of unsalted butter

1 coffee spoon of ground cumin

2 pounds of monkfish filet

½ cup olive oil

1 cup of mussel broth

Salt and freshly ground pepper to taste

Dill

Fresh chives, chopped, for garnish

Peel the potato and cut it into 8 equal pieces. Put it in a pan with garlic cloves with skin and add the heavy cream, salt and two teaspoons of water. Bring to a boil and let it cook covered for 10 to 15 minutes until the potato and garlic are fully cooked. Then transfer all in a strainer and push the potato and garlic mixture through the strainer to obtain a thick purée of garlic. Keep in refrigerator for at least 1 hour so that it cools down completely.

Clean the leeks and baby carrots. Slice the leeks in thick juliennes and make sure you wash the vegetable thoroughly before cooking. Cook the baby carrots for 5 minutes in boiling salted water and when finished, cool them down in ice water to keep their nice color and flavor.

Once the carrots are cool, sauté the leeks in butter and add the cumin powder and a pinch of salt. After 3 minutes add the baby carrots and let them cook together for another 2 minutes.

Roast the monkfish filet in olive oil and let the filets bake for a good 3 minutes on each side depending upon the thickness but make sure that the temperature is not too high. When finished baking one side turn the monkfish over and put a spoonful of garlic purée on top of each filet. Spread it evenly and cook the monkfish for another 2 minutes in a preheated oven at 350 degrees.

To finish sauce add some mussel broth to the vegetables while cooking. Add some freshly ground pepper and salt to taste.

Fry the dill in vegetable oil for 20 seconds and keep them on paper until using them as garnish.

Frederick De Pue
Executive Chef, European Union

Lacquered Braised Sea Bass with Ragout of Chanterelles

SERVES 4

2 ounces olive oil

1 onion, peeled and minced

1 clove garlic, peeled and minced

Chanterelles

2 slices prosciutto, minced

2 tablespoons coriander seeds

2 cups veal stock

2 cups fish stock

4 6-ounce filets of sea bass, skin on, center cut

4 ounces unsalted butter

Salt and pepper to taste

Preheat oven to 275 degrees. Heat 1 ounce oil over medium heat and sweat onions and garlic. Add chanterelles, prosciutto and coriander. Deglaze with veal and fish stock and place in oven for ½ hour. Remove from heat and keep warm.

Heat remaining oil. Season and sear sea bass on both sides until skin is crisp. Remove from pan and add sea bass to mushroom mixture. Brush sea bass with some of the reduced braising liquid and return to oven. Season and continue to braise until desired doneness. Remove from oven and transfer to parchment lined sheet pan. Reduce braising liquid to one cup. Finish with butter. Season to taste.

Design Cuisine

Shrimp Remoulade

SERVES 4 AS A FIRST COURSE

1 pound cooked shrimp

½ cup olive oil

¼ cup vinegar

1 teaspoon salt

1 teaspoon paprika

¼ teaspoon pepper

4 tablespoons mayonnaise

8 tablespoons Creole mustard

3 tablespoons finely chopped parsley

½ cup chopped celery

½ medium onion, chopped

Rub bowl with garlic. Mix all ingredients together. Blend well. Add shrimp and chill. Allow mixture to marinate several hours before serving, preferably overnight. It is advisable to taste sauce before adding shrimp as sometimes it needs a little more of this or that.

Creole mustard is the distinctive ingredient in this recipe and other types of mustard should not be substituted.

Gerson Nordlinger, Jr.
NSO Board Member

Golden Caviar with Belon Oysters Wrapped in Spinach Leaves

SERVES 1

6 Maine Belon oysters

6 impeccable spinach leaves

4 ounces golden caviar

Hazelnut oil

Excellent vinegar of your choice

Salt and freshly ground pepper

Shuck 6 oysters and keep their juice. Poach oysters in their juice for 3 seconds. Poach spinach leaves for 5 seconds in boiling salt water and dry on kitchen towel.

Toss oysters in hazelnut and vinegar dressing and wrap in spinach leaves. On a large plate place 5 small portions of caviar around plate and one in center; position wrapped oysters on top.

Chef Jean Louis Palladin
Jean-Louis Restaurant at The Watergate

La Salade de Poisson Marine (Marinated Fish Salad)

SERVES 6

1 pound fresh salmon

1 pound fresh sea scallops

Juice of 10 lemons

Juice of 2 limes

2 teaspoons salt

½ teaspoon freshly ground pepper

1 teaspoon chopped fresh coriander (optional)

1 teaspoon chopped fresh dill

1 head Boston lettuce

1 head Belgian endive

2 tablespoons chopped shallots (optional)

2 tablespoons chopped parsley (optional)

2 tablespoons chopped green onions or chives (optional)

Black caviar

6 teaspoons vegetable oil

"My father and I developed this recipe, using the wonderful seafood available here in the Chesapeake Bay area."

Slice salmon into slivers. Place salmon and scallops in separate, deep earthenware bowls. Sprinkle evenly with lemon and lime juices; season with salt, pepper, coriander and dill. Cover and marinate overnight in refrigerator.

Wash greens; dry completely. Place a bed of lettuce on each of 6 chilled salad plates. Spread 4 spears of endive over lettuce leaves to form an "x." Layer salmon over endive, then scallops. If desired, garnish with a combination of shallots, parsley, green onion or chives and top each with about 1 teaspoon of caviar. Pour about 1 teaspoon oil over each plate to moisten and glaze. Serve at once.

If scallops are large, slice before marinating.

Chef François Haeringer
L'Auberge Chez François Restaurant

Baked Mussels

SERVES 4 TO 6 AS MAIN COURSE

SERVES MORE AS AN APPETIZER

5 dozen mussels, scrubbed and debearded

2 tablespoons melted butter

¼ cup olive oil

1 cup bread crumbs

10 sprigs fresh parsley, chopped

3 cloves garlic, pressed

½ teaspoon red pepper (cayenne)

Salt and freshly ground pepper to taste

Scrub mussels and throw away any that have opened. Pile mussels on a foil-covered cookie sheet with enough foil to enclose mussels for baking.

Melt butter and oil and pour over mussels. Sprinkle bread crumbs, parsley, garlic, salt and peppers over mussels.

Cover mussels tightly with foil and bake in a 375 degree oven for 30 to 40 minutes or until shells are opened. Serve hot with French bread to mop up sauce.

Pat Vande Vort

Fisherman's Wharf Cioppino

SERVES 6 TO 8

1 pound cod, white fish or monk fish, cut into chunks

1 pound shrimp, peeled and rinsed

1 10-ounce can whole clams

2 large garlic cloves, pressed

1 large onion, chopped

1 green pepper, seeded and chopped

¼ pound fresh mushrooms, sliced

3 tablespoons fresh parsley, chopped

¼ cup olive oil

1 28-ounce can whole tomatoes, chopped

1 8-ounce bottle clam juice

1 chicken bouillon cube

2 cups dry red wine

⅓ cup tomato paste

1 teaspoon oregano, crumbled

½ teaspoon salt

¼ teaspoon pepper

Drain clams; reserving liquid. In a dutch oven, sauté garlic, onion, green pepper, mushrooms and parsley in olive oil. Add reserved calm liquid, tomatoes with liquid, clam juice, bouillon cube, wine, tomato paste and seasonings to sautéed vegetables. Simmer uncovered for 35 minutes. Add fish, shrimp and clams. Cook until heated through. If doubling the recipe, do not add any additional red wine.

Nancy Joan Crum
NSO Women's Committee Member

Oysters Rockefeller

SERVES 10 TO 12 AS AN APPETIZER

SERVES 4 AS A MAIN COURSE

MAKES 1 QUART OF SAUCE

1 bunch green onions

½ stalk celery

½ bunch parsley, leaves only

¼-½ cup broccoli heads, cooked and well drained

1 package (10 ounces) frozen leaf spinach, cooked and well drained

½ teaspoon anise seed

32 oysters

1½ cups (3 sticks) butter, melted

¼-½ cup toasted bread crumbs

2 tablespoons Worcestershire sauce

½ teaspoon salt

½ teaspoon freshly ground pepper

½ teaspoon red pepper

1 tablespoon Pernod (or similar absinthe liquor)

SAUCE

Chop, then grind all greens and anise seed in blender or food processor using melted butter as liquid. Transfer to a bowl and add bread crumbs, Worcestershire sauce, salt, pepper, red pepper and Pernod. Store in covered container in refrigerator where it will keep several days. Freezes well, but if you freeze, do not add Pernod until you defrost and are ready to serve.

TO SERVE

Place oysters in shells. Have oysters at room temperature if possible. Place shells on shallow pan and set in 400 degree oven. When edges of oysters begin to curl, remove and pour liquid from each shell. Cover oysters with Rockefeller sauce and return to oven until slightly brown.

It is best to seek out medium-size deep oyster shells for this dish. Ask your local fish merchant to save you some when he shucks his oysters.

Janet Perry, NSO Viola
and Richard Smith

Seafood Strudel

SERVES 4

½ cup fine bread crumbs

½ cup freshly grated Parmesan cheese

2 teaspoons dry mustard

1 very finely chopped onion

1 tablespoon butter

2 cups mixed seafood, cut in pieces (scallops, cooked lobster meat, cooked shrimp and/or crabmeat)

1½ cups sour cream

½ teaspoon salt

¼ teaspoon freshly cracked white pepper

2 tablespoons chives, chopped

2 tablespoons parsley, chopped

5 sheets phyllo dough

1 lemon

Melted Butter

Put bread crumbs, grated Parmesan cheese and dry mustard into a small bowl and mix well. Set aside. Cook onion in butter over high heat until transparent, but do not let it brown. Mix seafood with sour cream; add onion, salt, pepper, chives and parsley.

Work with phyllo sheets one sheet at a time, keeping the remaining sheets covered with a damp, not wet, towel. On a sheet of wax paper, stack the phyllo sheets, brushing each sheet with some of the melted butter before adding the next one over the first one. Brush the top sheet with melted butter, too, and sprinkle with the cheese-bread crumb mixture. Spoon seafood mixture one inch from one long edge of phyllo sheets, leaving a one-inch margin at each end.

Start rolling up the seafood in the pastry, folding in the ends as you roll, so that the seafood is wrapped securely inside the pastry roll. Use the wax paper to help you roll it. Place the roll on a baking sheet and brush it all over with melted butter.

Place it in a preheated 375 degree oven on the middle rack and bake for 30 minutes or until crisp and light brown. Slice 3 inches thick and serve hot with lemon butter, made by mixing remaining melted butter with the juice of a lemon.

Dr. Maria I. Wood
NSO Women's Committee Member

Gingered Shrimp

SERVES 6

4 teaspoons cornstarch, divided

½ teaspoon salt

1 pound small shrimp, shelled and deveined

1 large onion

1 large cucumber

½ cup chicken broth

2 tablespoons soy sauce

2 cloves crushed garlic

1½ teaspoons ground ginger

1 8½-ounce can water chestnuts, drained and sliced

½ tablespoon lemon juice

Lemon wedges, optional

Parsley, optional

Peanut or vegetable oil

In large bowl, sprinkle 3 teaspoons of the cornstarch and salt over the shrimp. Toss to coat. Refrigerate. Cut onion into wedges. Cut wedges crosswise in half. Cut cucumber in half, lengthwise. Cut crosswise into ¼ inch slices. In small cup combine chicken broth, soy sauce and remaining cornstarch.

In wok or large skillet, heat ¼ cup of oil. Add shrimp and stir-fry until pink, two or three minutes. Remove with slotted spoon and keep hot. Add onion, garlic and ginger to oil. Stir-fry one minute, adding more oil if needed. Add cucumber and stir-fry for two minutes. Add water chestnuts. Stir soy sauce mixture well, and stir rapidly into wok. Cook until sauce thickens and clings to vegetables, about four minutes. Return shrimp to wok. Cook until hot throughout. Stir in lemon juice. Garnish with lemon and parsley. Serve with rice, if desired.

Annette Rickel
NSO Board Member

Carolina Shrimp and Grits

SERVES 4

Shrimp and Grits are good for breakfast, lunch, brunch or dinner. They are a true reflection of the South Carolina Low Country and could very well be its signature recipe.

2 cups dry grits (Anson Mills blanched grits or Quaker quick grits)

2 cups water or chicken broth

¼ pound salt cured country ham (can substitute bacon or smoked cured ham)

1 large onion julienne

1 pound shrimp 21-25 (medium shrimp)

1 cup Madeira

3 cups heavy cream

1 tablespoon chopped fresh herbs (chives, parsley, chervil, basil, etc.)

Pepper to taste

Salt to taste

Butter

FOR THE GRITS

In a medium sauce pot heat 3 cups of water or chicken broth. When it comes to a boil add 2 cups of dry grits either Anson Mills blanched grits or Quaker quick grits. When grits begin to thicken add some milk to thin out a little and cook for about 10 minutes on slow heat. When the grits are creamy, add a touch of salt and pepper and a touch of butter.

FOR THE SHRIMP GRAVY

In a medium nonstick sauté pan caramelize the onions on low heat slowly so that you can achieve a nice golden brown. When caramelized add the country ham and continue to brown. Once the ham has become crispy, add the shrimp and sear them.

When the shrimp become slightly pink, deglaze the pan with the Madeira. Cook the Madeira half way down to cook off the alcohol; then add the heavy cream. Once the cream is added, cook at a simmer until thick. When the cream has reduced and become thick, season with some fresh cracked black pepper and the fresh cut herbs. If salt is needed use sparingly.

When carmelizing onions use low heat, and if they begin to burn add a little water and continue to cook.

Chef James Clark
Palette Restaurant

Saucisson de Crustaces

SERVES 4

3 ounces jumbo, all-lump crabmeat

3 ounces lobster meat

3 ounces crayfish tails (meat)

5 ounces bay scallops

1½ ounces Cognac

4 ounces salmon filet

4 ounces sea scallops

4 ounces heavy cream

1 egg

Salt, freshly ground pepper and nutmeg

Cognac

Pistachio nuts

2 feet of medium beef casing (available at Italian food specialty shops and custom butchers)

SAUCE

12 ounces of ripe tomatoes

1 teaspoon tomato paste

3 teaspoons red wine vinegar

1 cup virgin olive oil

Salt

Freshly ground pepper

Freshly chopped tarragon

Freshly chopped parsley

Sauté lobster, crabmeat and crayfish meat in butter and deglaze with Cognac. Allow to cool. Sauté bay scallops in butter until three quarters done. Cool.

Grind salmon filet and sea scallops. Place this in a food processor. Blend briefly. Add egg and blend. Add salt, pepper and nutmeg to taste. Add cream, a little at a time.

Mix sautéed and blended ingredients together and add pistachio nuts. Stuff this mixture in a medium beef casing. Poach at 180 degrees for 45 minutes. Cool.

Carefully cut sausage and arrange slices on plate over the following sauce.

SAUCE
Blanch tomatoes for 10 seconds in boiling water; then plunge into cold water. When they are chilled, peel and cut tomatoes in half and squeeze to remove seeds and water. Push tomato pulp through a fine sieve, pressing down on it with back of a wooden spoon. Collect tomato purée in a bowl and refrigerate until ready to use.

Add tomato paste and vinegar to sieved tomatoes. Mixing continuously with a wire whisk, incorporate oil, a few drops at a time. Add salt, pepper, tarragon and parsley.

Chef Pierre Chambrin
Maison Blanche Restaurant

Mussels with Saffron

SERVES 6

4 pounds mussels, scrubbed and debearded

2 cups heavy cream

5 shallots, chopped

2 cups white wine

2 pinches of saffron

10 ounces mushrooms, sliced

3 carrots, julienned

2 zucchini, julienned

½ teaspoon freshly ground pepper

Steam open mussels with white wine, pepper and shallots. Remove and shell mussels. Strain and reserve broth.

Simmer carrots slowly in butter until tender. Separately sauté mushrooms and zucchini rapidly to retain crispness.

Add saffron to broth and reduce. Then add heavy cream and reduce again to an even creamier consistency. Add mussels and vegetables. Bring to a slow boil and serve.

Chef Garard Vettraino
Jean-Pierre Restaurant

Shrimp Madeleine

SERVES 8

2 tablespoons dry English mustard

4 tablespoons butter

3 pounds raw shrimp, medium size

⅓ cup brandy

2 cups heavy cream

Salt and freshly ground pepper

Mix dry mustard with a little water to make a light paste. Melt butter over high heat and sauté shrimp until all water has evaporated. Remove from heat. Then pour brandy over shrimp and ignite.

When flames subside, add cream and cook, stirring all the time, until a smooth sauce is obtained. Add mustard paste and season to taste with salt and pepper. Serve in individual casserole dishes or on a platter; garnish with parsley.

Chef Roland Huet
Christian's Restaurant, New Orleans

Coquilles St. Jacques Baumanière

SERVES 4 TO 6 AS A MAIN COURSE

♪

This is an easy and delightful dish to prepare. The scallops come out very tender. May serve as a first course.

1½ pounds scallops (if sea scallops, cut in quarters)

4 tablespoons softened butter

1 tablespoon chopped shallots

1 teaspoon salt

Dash of white pepper

½ cup dry vermouth

1 cup heavy cream

1 tablespoon flour

Minced fresh parsley

4-6 scallop shells for serving

Wash scallops and quarter, if necessary. Put scallops in a saucepan and add shallots, salt, white pepper and vermouth. Bring this to a boil, then cover pan and simmer for 2 minutes.

Remove scallops, using a slotted spoon and place in scallop shells. Remaining liquid should be cooked over a light flame until it is reduced by half.

To make sauce, add cream to liquid in saucepan and boil rapidly until syrupy. Then, to this add flour and butter, stirring butter over a low flame.

Pour sauce over scallops and sprinkle parsley over top. Heat scallops in a 450 degree oven for 5 minutes and they are ready to serve.

Guest Conductor, Erich Leinsdorf
Version of Hotel de la Poste's recipe, Burgundy, France

Associate Principal Viola William Foster teaches a young student on the NSO's North Dakota Residency (2003). Credit Scott Suchman.

Note: *recipes marked with this icon are from the original National Symphony Orchestra Cookbook, published by FANS (Friends Assisting the National Symphony) in 1983.*

POULTRY & GAME

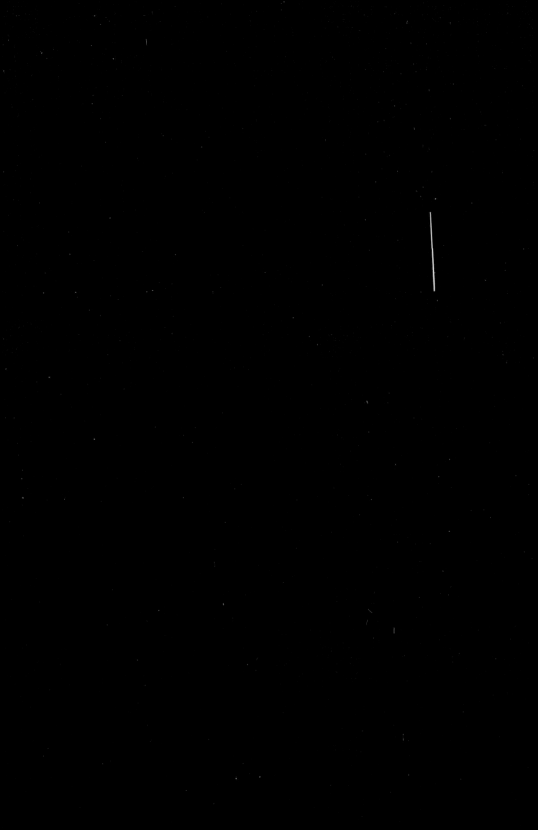

POULTRY & GAME

Arroz Con Pollo (Chicken with Rice)

SERVES 6
♪

3-pound frying chicken or combination of favorite parts

½ cup olive oil

2 cups minced onions

3 cloves garlic

½ teaspoon red pepper

2½ teaspoons salt

1½ cups yellow or regular rice

28-ounce can tomatoes, undrained and chopped

10¾-ounce can chicken broth

5 ounces frozen peas

½ cup stuffed green olives

4-ounce jar sliced pimentos

Heat olive oil in large, heavy pan and brown chicken on both sides.

Remove chicken. Sauté onion, garlic, and red pepper about 3 minutes (onion will be golden).

Add rice, salt and pepper and stir until rice is browned (about 8 minutes). Add tomatoes and chicken broth to rice mixture and stir.

Add chicken, cover pan and simmer for 1 hour.

Add ½ cup water and stir. Add peas, olives and pimentos, placing them on top. Simmer 20 minutes or until peas are cooked. Serve from pan.

Luis Haza
NSO First Violin

Baja California Chicken

SERVES 8

8 boned chicken breasts

Seasoned salt and freshly ground pepper to taste

2 cloves garlic, crushed

4 tablespoons olive oil

4 tablespoons tarragon vinegar

⅔ cup dry sherry

Sprinkle chicken with seasoned salt and pepper.

Crush garlic into oil and vinegar in a skillet. Sauté chicken pieces until golden brown, turning frequently. Remove; place in baking dish.

Pour sherry over pieces and place in 350 degree oven for 10 minutes.

Mrs. Ronald W. Reagan
Former First Lady

Chicken with Lamb and Rice

SERVES 6

3 whole chicken breasts

⅓ cup pine nuts, toasted lightly

1 cup ground lamb (½ pound)

2 tablespoons butter, melted

1 cup rice

½ cup toasted, slivered almonds

Salt, freshly ground pepper and allspice

1 bay leaf

½ teaspoon coriander

Poach breasts in water with bay leaf and coriander for 10 minutes. Let cool in broth, debone and cut into 2-inch squares. Reserve broth. In a frying pan, sauté lamb until no longer pink.

In a saucepan, combine lamb, pine nuts, rice, salt, pepper, allspice and melted butter. Add 2 cups hot reserved broth. Cover and simmer 15 minutes.

Add chicken. Simmer 5 minutes longer.

To serve, mound rice on large platter; cover rice mixture with chicken and sprinkle with toasted almonds.

Leftovers may be turned into a very good cold salad by adding dressing to chilled mixture.

Embassy of Lebanon

Chicken Moghlai

SERVES 8

8 whole chicken breasts, skinned, boned and halved

Salt and freshly ground pepper to taste

Flour

½ cup butter

4 medium onions, chopped

4 garlic cloves, minced

1 tablespoon minced ginger

½ teaspoon cumin powder

½ teaspoon turmeric

¼ teaspoon cumin seeds

¼ teaspoon caraway seeds

¼ teaspoon cayenne

1 canned whole green chili, minced

1-pound can whole, peeled tomatoes, undrained

2 cups chicken stock or broth

2 pints sour cream

½ cup brown sugar

1 teaspoon saffron threads

½ teaspoon ground cardamom

¼ teaspoon ground cloves

¼ teaspoon nutmeg

2 tablespoons ketchup

2-3 teaspoons dried red pepper flakes

Chopped cilantro (as garnish)

Place chicken on cookie sheet. Season very generously with salt and lightly sprinkle with pepper. Dust thoroughly with flour.

Melt ¼ cup butter in 14-inch skillet. Brown half the breasts until golden on both sides. Remove and set aside. Add additional ¼ cup butter and brown remaining breasts. Set aside. Add onions to skillet and sauté over medium heat until soft. Stir in garlic and ginger and cook 2 minutes.

Add cumin powder, turmeric, cumin seeds, caraway seeds, cayenne and chili. Stir in tomatoes, mashing with wooden spoon. Blend in chicken stock. Return chicken to pan and bring to boil. Reduce heat and simmer uncovered for 8 to 10 minutes.

Combine remaining ingredients except cilantro. Slowly stir into chicken mixture. Cook, covered, over low heat 30 minutes. Uncover and cook 45 minutes more, stirring frequently. Season to taste with salt and more red pepper flakes, if desired. Place in serving bowl and garnish with cilantro.

The sauce will have a curdled appearance, which is proper with this recipe. The texture will be smooth to the taste, however. Excellent cooked in advance and reheated.

Mrs. Zubin Mehta
Wife of Guest Conductor, Zubin Mehta

Chicken Parmigiana

SERVES 4

4 whole, chicken breasts. skinned and boned

⅓ cup butter

1 egg

1 cup seasoned bread crumbs

15½-ounce jar spaghetti sauce or your own homemade

2 cloves garlic, crushed

½ teaspoon thyme

½ teaspoon oregano

8-ounce box thin spinach noodles, cooked

6 slices mozzarella cheese

5 ounces grated Parmesan cheese

Cut chicken breasts in half. Rinse in cold water and pat dry. Pound with a meat mallet until ¼ inch thick.

Heat butter in a large skillet. Beat egg in a medium bowl. Dip chicken in beaten egg and then into 1 cup seasoned bread crumbs.

Sauté chicken in butter, 2 minutes on each side. Pour spaghetti sauce into same pan. Add garlic, thyme and oregano. Bring to a boil; cover and reduce to simmer for 20 minutes.

Place a slice of mozzarella cheese on top of each piece of chicken 5 minutes before end of cooking time. Sprinkle grated Parmesan cheese on top. Cover skillet.

Drain cooked noodles and place on a warmed serving platter with chicken on top.

Peggy Ahlfeld

Chicken Piquant

SERVES 4

This recipe was selected by the Inaugural Committee as the entrée to serve President Reagan at the first Inaugural Luncheon in the Capital Rotunda.

2 whole chicken breasts, skinned and boned

4 tablespoons butter

¼ cup flour

5 tablespoons capers

⅓ cup dry white wine

Salt and freshly ground pepper to taste

Cut chicken into strips. Melt butter in pan. Coat chicken in seasoned flour and sauté in melted butter until golden brown.

Deglaze chicken with white wine and capers. Reduce liquid to desired thickness. Season to taste. Serve with a garnish of chopped parsley.

Mrs. William French Smith

Germaine's Lemon Chicken

SERVES 4 TO 6

2-3 chicken breasts split, boned and skinned

White pepper and salt to taste

1 tablespoon pale dry sherry

¾ cup fresh lemon juice

1 egg white

½ cup all-purpose flour

½ cup cornstarch

½ cup water

1 cup shredded iceberg lettuce

1 tomato, sliced for garnish

½ lemon, sliced for garnish

2 tablespoons vegetable oil

4 tablespoons ketchup

2 tablespoons soy sauce

1 tablespoon sesame oil

3 tablespoons sugar

¼ teaspoon ginger, chopped

½ teaspoon garlic, chopped

½ teaspoon chili and garlic paste (optional)

1 teaspoon roasted sesame seeds

1 teaspoon scallion, chopped

Pour mixture of pepper, salt and sherry, and all but 3 tablespoons of lemon juice over chicken. Let marinate for 30 to 40 minutes.

Mix egg white, flour, cornstarch and water. Coat pieces of chicken with this mixture and deep fry until light golden brown over medium heat. Drain and cut into bite-size pieces.

Arrange chicken, lettuce, tomato and lemon on plate.

Heat vegetable oil. Add ketchup, soy sauce, sesame oil, remaining lemon juice, sugar, ginger and garlic (and chili or garlic paste). Stir until just hot. Pour over chicken before serving. Sprinkle with scallion and sesame seeds.

Germaine Swanson
Germaine's Restaurant

Louise's Chicken Alouette

SERVES 4

1 container Alouette or Boursin cheese

2 whole boneless chicken breasts

2 eggs, beaten

1 cup bread crumbs

½ cup melted butter

Fresh parsley

Split chicken breasts and flatten between pieces of wax paper.

Cut cheese into four parts. Roll cheese into cylinder shape, place cheese in middle of chicken breast, and roll breast around cheese.

Dip rolled-up chicken breast in egg; then roll in bread crumbs. Place in baking dish seam side down. Cover with melted butter.

Bake at 350 degrees for 20 to 30 minutes, basting occasionally. Garnish with fresh parsley.

Louise Millikan
Former NSO FANS Member

Poulet au Vinaigre

SERVES 4

2 chickens (broilers), 2 pounds each

2 carrots

1 stick celery

2 tomatoes

2 tablespoons oil

½ pound sweet butter

4 tablespoons red wine vinegar

½ cup white wine

2 cloves garlic, mashed

Chopped parsley or tarragon

Salt and freshly ground pepper

Cut chicken in quarters. Season to taste. Cut carrots and celery in small pieces. Peel, seed and slice tomatoes.

Sauté chicken with 2 tablespoons oil and 3 tablespoons butter. Brown on both sides. Add carrots and celery; sauté for 5 more minutes. Add vinegar, white wine, garlic and tomatoes. Cover and cook for 25 minutes slowly.

Remove chicken from pan and place on serving dish. Reduce cooking liquid. Season and add 4 tablespoons butter. Pour over chicken and sprinkle with fresh tarragon or chopped parsley.

Chef Jean-Pierre Goyenvalle
Le Lion d'Or Restaurant

Puffed Chicken Pockets

SERVES 8

1 box Pepperidge Farm Puff Pastry, thawed

6 ounces cream cheese

6 tablespoons melted butter

4 cups chicken, cooked and cubed

4 tablespoons milk

½ teaspoon salt

¼ teaspoon freshly ground pepper

2 tablespoons chopped pimento

1½ cups bread crumbs

1-2 tablespoons fresh dill, chopped (optional)

Blend cream cheese and 4 tablespoons butter. Add chicken, salt, pepper, milk, pimentos and dill.

Thaw frozen puff pastries; roll out each sheet to yield 9, 3-inch squares. (One box of 2 sheets will yield 18 dough squares.) Place 1 to 2 tablespoons of chicken mixture in center of each square and pinch opposing sides together at center.

Baste with remaining butter. Roll in bread crumbs. Bake at 350 degrees for 35 minutes, or until squares are puffed and brown. Serve hot.

These chicken squares can be made ahead and stored unbaked frozen. You do not need to thaw before baking.

Cookbook Committee

Chicken with Apricots

SERVES 6

1 pound dried apricots

4 cups water

2 onions, minced

4 pounds chicken, cut up

2 tablespoons olive oil

1½ teaspoons salt

1 tablespoon lemon juice

2 tablespoons brown sugar

1 teaspoon cinnamon

Wash the apricots and soak in the water for one hour. Brown the onions and the chicken in the olive oil. Add the salt, lemon juice, sugar, cinnamon and undrained apricots. Cover and cook over low heat 2½ hours or until chicken is tender.

Best made one day before eating. Refrigerate overnight. Skim visible fat before reheating.

Alice Kogan Weinreb
NSO Flute

Roasted Chicken

SERVES 2 TO 3

1 free-range roasting chicken

1½ tablespoons unsalted butter, softened

Sea salt

Freshly ground black pepper

Paprika

4 whole heads fresh garlic, unpeeled, cut in half horizontally

6 sprigs fresh rosemary

6 sprigs fresh thyme

Rainwater Madeira and water

Preheat oven to 425 degrees. Rub the skin of the chicken with the butter; season it well with the salt, pepper and paprika.

Place the chicken on its side in an ovenproof baking dish. Place the halved garlic heads, cut side up, around the pan. Lay the rosemary and thyme on top of the chicken. Put the baking dish in the center of the oven and roast, uncovered, for 20 minutes.

Add ¼ cup water, turn the chicken on its other side and roast another 20 minutes.

Turn the chicken breast side up. Add ½ cup Madeira and roast another 20 minutes. Total roasting time should be 1 hour. By now the skin should be a golden color. Reduce heat to 400 degrees and roast 15 minutes more.

After taking the chicken out of the oven, turn it to rest with its tail in the air. This makes the bird perfectly moist, as the juices flow down through the breast meat. (When you roast a chicken breast side up only, the delicate white meat dries out.) Let it rest for 10 minutes or more.

When serving, spoon sauce over the chicken pieces. Garnish the chicken with roasted garlic on warmed plates.

Serve with small red potatoes and green beans.

Cookbook Committee

Honey-Soy Braised Chicken

SERVES 4

8 chicken thighs, skinned

2 tablespoons oil

SAUCE
⅓ cup soy sauce

2 tablespoons honey

2 tablespoons sake

1 clove garlic, minced

½ teaspoon fresh ginger, grated

Heat oil in deep skillet. Fry chicken thighs on high heat 3 to 4 minutes, turning once, until lightly browned on the outside.

Combine sauce ingredients and pour over chicken. Cover and simmer for 30 minutes, turning once.

Toshiko Kohno
NSO Principal Flute

Summer and Spice Chicken

SERVES 4

Juice of 1 lemon

1½ -2 pounds boneless chicken breasts, cut into small cubes

Salt and freshly ground pepper to taste

1 tablespoon oil

1 cup yogurt

1 teaspoon chili powder or to taste

Raw vegetables (carrots, cucumbers, red or green peppers, cauliflower, broccoli, jicama or your choice) cut in sticks or slices for serving

Set aside 1 tablespoon lemon juice for dip and toss rest with chicken cubes. Then toss chicken with salt, pepper and oil. Set aside.

In a small serving bowl combine yogurt with reserved lemon juice, chili powder, salt and pepper to taste. Set aside (can be refrigerated and kept a week or more).

Thread chicken on small bamboo skewers. Grill skewers of chicken, preferably on a charcoal grill, for about 10 to 15 minutes, turning as it cooks, just until meat is opaque. Arrange on serving platter with raw vegetables and yogurt sauce. Dip chicken and vegetables in yogurt as you eat them.

Phyllis Richman
Former Food Critic, The Washington Post

Sautéed Boursin Chicken Breasts

SERVES 4

4-5 ounces garlic and herb-flavored Boursin cheese

4 halved chicken breasts, skinned and boned

Lime juice

Salt and pepper

2 eggs

Flour

Dry bread crumbs

2 ounces butter

¼ cup oil

Several hours or the day before, bring cheese to room temperature. Lay chicken breasts on a cookie sheet and remove tendons. Freeze for about 10 minutes, or until firm to the touch. Cut them in half horizontally, but not quite through to the opposite side, so that breasts open like a book. Flatten the butterflied breasts lightly for even thickness.

Spread a quarter of the cheese over half of each breast, leaving about ¾ inch around edges. Close the halves and press lightly. Sprinkle breasts with a little lime juice, salt and pepper. In shallow dish beat eggs and coat with crumbs. Refrigerate for at least an hour, or overnight.

In heavy skillet, just large enough to hold chicken in one layer, sauté breast in butter and oil for 3 to 4 minutes on each side. Transfer to paper towels for a moment to drain. Serve immediately.

—
Bea Welters
NSO Board Member

Chicken Curry

SERVES 6

10 boneless, skinless chicken breasts

½-¾ cup olive oil

1 cup finely chopped celery

1 cup finely chopped onion

3 tablespoons curry powder

4 medium size apples, pared and chopped

⅛ teaspoon cayenne pepper

½ teaspoon salt, optional

Fresh ground pepper

Sauté chicken in oil for 10 minutes or until brown. Remove chicken and keep warm. Add celery and onion to oil remaining in skillet and sauté for 5 minutes. Add all other ingredients. Then, add water, just enough to create enough sauce for chicken. Cover and simmer for 30 to 40 minutes.

Serve over fluffy rice. Condiments can be added when serving.

—
Noémi K. Neidorff
NSO National Trustee

Carol's Baked Chicken Cutlets

SERVES 4

4-8 skinless chicken cutlets (breast meat)

Beaten eggs

Bread crumbs

Chicken broth, canned or fresh

½-1 pound mushrooms, sliced

Salt and pepper to taste

Butter

White wine or sherry (optional)

Dip cutlets first into beaten egg and then into bread crumbs (Tip: Put beaten egg and bread crumbs into separate plastic bags. Drop cutlet into egg, remove and then drop into bread crumbs).

Sauté in hot butter until browned on both sides. Add additional butter as necessary. Remove from pan. Deglaze pan with chicken broth (about 1 cup). Sauté mushrooms in butter and add to sauce. Season to taste. Add wine or sherry if desired.

Put layer of sauce in shallow pan or ovenproof dish, place chicken cutlets on top and bake until thoroughly heated, approximately 30 minutes. Serve with additional sauce.

Virginia C. Mars
NSO Board Member

Mango and Mustard Chicken

SERVES 6

6 chicken breasts

1 tablespoon mango chutney

1 tablespoon Worcestershire sauce

1 tablespoon lemon juice

1 tablespoon apricot jam

½ cup mayonnaise

2 teaspoons grainy mustard

Put the chicken breasts in an ovenproof dish. In a bowl combine jam, chutney, mayonnaise, Worcestershire sauce, mustard and lemon juice. Pour over chicken. Cover dish with aluminum foil and leave to marinate for several hours. Cook covered for 35 minutes at 250 degrees.

Gillian Von Drehle
NSO Women's Committee Member

Chicken Couscous

SERVES 8

4 large skinless, boneless chicken breasts (or 6 skinless, boneless thighs), cut into bite-sized pieces

¼ cup olive oil

4 large carrots, thickly sliced

1 large onion, sliced

6 cups chicken broth

3 cinnamon sticks

10 cloves or ¼ teaspoon ground cloves

1-2 teaspoons conserie d'harissa, use to taste-it's hot

½ teaspoon salt to taste

½ teaspoon pepper to taste

4 tomatoes, cut up, or 1 large can plum tomatoes, cut up, including liquid from can

1 can garbanzo beans, drained

½ cup raisins

3 zucchini, cut into 2-inch pieces

1 box plain couscous

CONSERIE D'HARISSA

2 tablespoons cayenne pepper

1 tablespoon cumin

2 garlic cloves, minced

½ teaspoon salt

CONSERIE D'HARISSA

Mash together cayenne pepper, cumin, garlic cloves and salt. Use a mortar and pestle if available. Set aside.

CHICKEN COUSCOUS

In a large stew pot sauté chicken in olive oil; then add carrots and onion. Cover with chicken broth and simmer for 20 minutes.

To the pot add cinnamon sticks, cloves, 1 to 2 teaspoons conserie d'harissa, salt and pepper. Then add 4 cut up tomatoes or 1 large can of plum tomatoes which have been cut up. If using the canned plum tomatoes, include the liquid as well. Cook for an additional 40 minutes.

Add garbanzo beans, raisins and zucchini. Cook 30 minutes longer. Remove cloves and cinnamon sticks.

If possible, prepare ahead and refrigerate overnight. Prepare couscous according to the package instructions. Reheat stew; pour over couscous in wide bowl and serve.

Rita Shapiro
NSO Executive Director

Poulet Marinade

SERVES 6

3 whole skinned and boned chicken breasts

3 medium garlic cloves, minced

½ cup brown sugar

3 tablespoons whole grain Dijon mustard

¾ cup cider

Juice of one lemon

Juice of one lime

6 tablespoons olive oil

1 teaspoon ground pepper

Thoroughly wash and pat dry the chicken breasts. Slice breasts in half lengthwise. In large bowl, mix all remaining ingredients and marinate the chicken breasts for one hour at room temperature. If time permits, marinate in the refrigerator for at least 8 hours.

On an outdoor or indoor grill or grilling skillet, cook the chicken breasts for 5 to 7 minutes on each side. If using a grilling skillet, be sure to cook the breasts on high heat. May be garnished with lemon and parsley.

Annette Rickel
NSO Board Member

Aegean Chicken

SERVES 6

7 boneless chicken breasts, cut into bite-size pieces

Flour to dredge chicken

9 ounces marinated artichoke hearts (liquid reserved)

¼ cup olive oil

3 tablespoons butter

½ pound mushrooms

22 ounces Italian canned tomatoes with liquid

3 cloves garlic, minced

¾ cup black olives

1 teaspoons salt

¼ teaspoon dried oregano

½ teaspoon dried basil

¾ teaspoon black pepper

¾ cup sherry

Dredge chicken pieces in flour. Sauté them in liquid from artichoke hearts and olive oil. Remove from pan and sauté mushrooms, adding butter if needed. Remove to separate bowl. Add tomatoes, garlic, olives and all seasonings to pan. Simmer 10 minutes. Add chicken, reserved artichokes and sherry. Simmer 10 more minutes and add mushrooms.

Carole Ash
The Artful Party

Cornish Hen Broiled with Lemon-Garlic Butter

SERVES 6

3 Cornish hens, halved

¼ pound sweet butter, softened

1 teaspoon lemon juice

½ teaspoon garlic, finely chopped

2 tablespoons coarse salt (sea salt)

Fresh black pepper

4 tablespoons parsley, finely chopped

Preheat broiler for 15 minutes. Wash hens quickly under cold water. (Halve them either before or after.) Dry well with paper towels.

Cream the butter with an electric beater. When it is very smooth, beat in the lemon juice a couple of drops at a time. Now add the garlic.

With a pastry brush, brush the hens with as much butter as they will hold and reserve the rest (if any is left) for basting. Lay the hens skin side down on the broiler rack. Grind some black pepper over them and sprinkle them evenly with one tablespoon of sea salt.

Broil the hens about 15 minutes on one side and 10 minutes on the other. (You do not want the outsides to char before the insides have begun to cook.)

Baste the hens frequently, every 5 minutes. After 15 minutes, turn the hens over carefully, do not break the skin. Baste thoroughly, sprinkle with a little pepper and the remaining tablespoon of salt and broil the hens skin side up for 10 minutes. Baste again; the skin should be kept moistened.

Remove birds to a hot platter. Scrape up the drippings and brown crust that clings to the broiling pan. Pour this over the hens and sprinkle chopped parsley on top.

To test for doneness, pierce the fleshy part of one of the legs with the point of a sharp knife. The juice that spurts out should be clear yellow. If it is tinged with pink, return them to the broiler for a few more minutes.

To assure that you have enough of the lemon-garlic butter, you could double the ingredients.

Cookbook Committee

Chicken Enchiladas

MAKES 15 ENCHILADAS

Cooking oil

2 4-ounce cans chopped green chilies

1 large clove garlic, minced

1 28-ounce can tomatoes

2 cups chopped onion

2 teaspoons salt

½ teaspoon oregano

3 cups shredded, cooked chicken

2 cups dairy sour cream

2 cups grated cheddar cheese

15 corn or flour tortillas

Preheat oil in skillet. Sauté chopped chilies with minced garlic in oil. Drain and break up tomatoes; reserve ½ cup liquid. To chilies and garlic, add tomatoes, onion, 1 teaspoon salt, oregano and reserved tomato liquid. Simmer uncovered until thick, about 30 minutes. Remove from skillet and set aside.

Combine chicken with sour cream, grated cheese and other teaspoon salt. Heat ⅓ cup oil; dip tortillas in oil until they become limp. Drain well on paper towels. Fill tortillas with chicken mixture; roll up and arrange side by side, seam down, in 9x13-inch baking dish. Pour tomato mixture over enchiladas and bake at 350 degrees until heated through, about 20 minutes.

President Bill Clinton
Former President of the United States

Taming the Wild Goose

SERVES 4

Chesapeake Bay wild goose

Onions

Celery

Carrots

Potatoes

Garlic

Red table wine

Clean and chop vegetables, except garlic. Rub inside and outsides of bird with garlic. Put vegetables in cavity. Place goose breast up on rack over shallow pan (at least 2½ to 3 inches above pan; bird should not touch drippings).

Cook at 170 degrees for 12 to 14 hours until drumstick moves easily. Baste frequently with wine and juices. Slow cooking does not dry out goose. When finished, discard vegetables.

Gravy can be made with red wine, drippings, and sautéed mushrooms. Serve with wild rice. Sherry or currant jelly sauce also make an excellent accompaniment to wild game.

G. Stuart Scott
Former NSO FANS Member

Roast Pheasants and Other Birds

SERVES 4

2 pheasants

Onion, celery, carrot and parsley

Butter for roasting birds

2 strips bacon

Lemon pepper

SAUCE

1 small jar currant jelly

1 cup dry sherry

½ cup (1 stick) butter

Rinse birds thoroughly and pat dry. Salt and lemon pepper the cavity and stuff with onion, celery, carrot and parsley. Dot liberally with butter and put bacon over breasts and high part of legs to prevent drying out.

Melt butter and jelly in saucepan. Remove from heat and add sherry. Make more than you will use for basting to use as gravy.

Roast at 350 degrees for 1½ hours (1 hour for quail; 2 hours for goose). Baste every 10 minutes with pan juices and sauce.

Reheat reserved sauce for gravy. It is important not to add pan juices to gravy sauce as they tend to be very gamey.

Recipe also works well with quail, duck and goose.

Anne Watson
Former NSO FANS Member

Tanqueray Turkey

SERVES 6 TO 8

Excellent diet dish! If you are not on a diet, it is especially good for sandwiches with chutney.

4-6 pound turkey breast (or whole turkey)

1 tablespoon curry powder

1 tablespoon fine herbs

1 teaspoon salt or salt substitute

1 teaspoon paprika

1 cup water

1 cup gin

1 orange, cut in half

1 onion

2 carrots

2 pieces of celery

Wash and dry turkey. Mix curry powder, herbs, salt and paprika. Rub turkey inside and out with this mixture.

Place in pan with vegetables and orange. Roast uncovered at 350 degrees for 3 hours. Baste with gin and water. When done, spoon off all fat from juices. Serve thinly sliced with pan juices.

Mrs. Donald L. Rogers

Fruit Stuffing for Turkey or Goose

MAKES ABOUT 2 QUARTS OF STUFFING

1 cup chopped, soft, pitted, dried prunes

¾ cup chopped, dried apricots

6 cups day-old bread cubes

2 cups cut-up, peeled apples

¾ cup diced orange sections

½ cup chopped nuts (optional)

1 teaspoon salt

½ teaspoon poultry seasoning

½ cup orange juice

¼ cup melted butter

Pour boiling water over first 2 ingredients; then drain. Toss lightly with remaining ingredients.

Fred Begun
Former NSO Principal Timpani

National Symphony Orchestra Concert in Red Square, Moscow, Russia (1993). Credit Joan Marcus.

Note: *recipes marked with this icon are from the original National Symphony Orchestra Cookbook, published by FANS (Friends Assisting the National Symphony) in 1983.*

BEEF

Brisket

SERVES 12 TO 15

5-pound brisket

8 onions, sliced

Prune juice (6 pack of small cans)

Pitted prunes

Small potatoes

Carrots

Garlic Powder

Salt and pepper

Paprika

Bay leaf

Preheat oven to 450 degrees. Cover bottom of pan with 6 sliced onions. Season brisket, add to pan and add more onions on top. Add prune juice. Cover. Cook 20 minutes. Turn heat down to 350 degrees and bake another 2 hours.

Add potatoes, carrots and prunes. Cook covered 1½ hours more (the last 10 minutes uncovered). Total baking time should be 3½ to 4 hours.

Susan Porter
NSO Board Member

Cordon Rouge

SERVES 6 TO 8

1 tenderloin of beef (size depending on number of people: ½ pound per person)

8 ounces pâté de foie gras

Smoked bacon strips

Salt and freshly ground pepper

In a heavy casserole, sear meat on all sides briefly over high heat. Remove meat and make an incision lengthwise, so meat opens like a book. Put slices of goose liver in opening. Close up. Season well with salt and pepper on outside and wrap meat with slices of smoked bacon. Secure this with string at 3 inch intervals.

Return wrapped tenderloin to pan and cook over high heat until bacon is browned and crisped. Remove bacon and string before slicing meat.

Serve Cordon Rouge with French fries, baby peas and artichoke hearts.

Anne-Sophie Mutter
Violinist, Guest Artist

Svíčková (Tenderloin of Beef in Sour Cream Sauce)

SERVES 4 TO 6

3 pounds tenderloin of beef

3-6 ounces of bacon

2 cups sliced vegetables (onion, carrot, parsnip and celery root)

½ cup butter

Salt and freshly ground pepper to taste

1 cup or more beef bouillon

8 peppercorns

8 whole allspice

1 bay leaf

Pinch of thyme

Flour

1 cup or more sour cream

Lingonberries

Lard meat with ½-inch thick bacon strips.

Brown vegetables in butter, add meat and brown on all sides. Pour in hot bouillon, salt and seasonings. Roast in a 325 degree oven until tender (1 to 1½ hours), basting frequently.

Remove meat from pan, dust drippings with flour. Add more bouillon if needed and simmer for 5 minutes.

Blend in sour cream and put sauce through a food processor to make creamy.

Serve with dumplings and wild lingonberries in sugar.

Rudolf Firkušný
Guest Conductor

Roast Filet of Beef

SERVES 8

3-3½ pounds filet of beef, trimmed, tied, dried with paper towel, seasoned

2 tablespoons vegetable oil

2 tablespoons butter

Salt and pepper

Heat vegetable oil and butter in a skillet large enough to hold the filet. When hot, sear the meat for a few minutes on each side until nicely browned. (The filet may be prepared ahead of time to this point and refrigerated.)

When ready to roast, let meat reach room temperature. Preheat oven to 400 degrees. Roast filet for 35 minutes at 400 degrees. Allow meat to rest before carving. Cover lightly with aluminum foil.

Cookbook Committee

Green Peppercorn Steak

SERVES 4

4 New York strip steaks

2 tablespoons vegetable oil

5 tablespoons butter

1 tablespoon minced shallots

½ cup beef bouillon

⅓ cup brandy

2-3 tablespoons green peppercorns

Dry steaks; pound with green peppercorns; allow several hours to set.

Heat 2 tablespoons of butter and 2 tablespoons vegetable oil, add steaks and cook rapidly on both sides (approximately 2 minutes on each side). Remove from pan; keep warm.

Sauté shallots, add bouillon and boil down rapidly. Add ⅓ cup brandy. Turn off heat, adding 3 tablespoons butter, one at a time. Pour sauce over steaks and serve immediately.

Mrs. Stephen Montgomery
Former NSO FANS Member

Flank Steak

SERVES 4

6 tablespoons golden brown mustard

2 cloves garlic, pressed through a garlic press ·

1 tablespoon freshly ground pepper

1-1½ pounds flank steak

Combine the mustard, garlic and pepper and using a pastry brush coat both sides of the steak with the mix. Heat an outside grill at least 20 minutes in advance of cooking so that it becomes as hot as possible.

Place the flank steak on the grill and cook approximately 4 minutes per side. Brush the steak with any of the remaining mustard mix during the grilling process.

When done, place the steak on the cutting board, cut thin slices on the diagonal and serve.

Patti Sowalsky

Steaks with Two Mustards

SERVES 2

2 small steaks, rib eye or Delmonico, well trimmed

1 tablespoon butter

1 tablespoon olive oil

2 ounces dry vermouth

2 tablespoons Worcestershire sauce

2 teaspoons tarragon mustard

2 teaspoons Dijon mustard

2 medium cloves garlic, pressed or finely chopped

Put butter and oil in a sauté pan or heavy skillet; heat over high flame to sizzling. Add steaks; sauté 1 to 2 minutes per side or until cooked to taste. Remove and set aside, keeping warm.

Deglaze pan with vermouth. Add Worcestershire sauce and reduce to 1 to 2 tablespoons. Press garlic into pan, cook a few seconds and then add mustards. Stir; cook for a couple of minutes over lowered heat.

Add steaks and accumulated juices and turn in the sauce. Serve immediately.

Wayne B. Swift
Former NSO FANS Member

Texas Chile Con Carne

SERVES 6 TO 8

1 green pepper, chopped fine

2 large onions, chopped fine

1 clove garlic, chopped fine

1 tablespoon butter or olive oil

3-4 tablespoons chili powder

2 tablespoons flour

1 teaspoon oregano

1 teaspoon ground cumin

2 pounds ground beef

1 21-ounce can tomatoes

1 cup water

2 tablespoons sugar

2 teaspoons salt

1 square unsweetened chocolate

2 15-ounce cans kidney beans

Fry onion, green pepper and garlic in fat until golden brown and transparent. Mix chili powder, flour and all herbs together and stir into onion mix. Cook 3 minutes; then add tomatoes and water. Simmer and season with sugar, salt and chocolate; stir until dissolved and cook 1 hour longer. The sauce should be about like gravy. It may be thinned with water and tomato sauce.

Brown beef and add sauce. Cook about 1 hour. Add beans and cook until blended.

Cathy Tennyson
Former NSO FANS Member

Brains Vinaigrette

SERVES 2-3

♩

"United Nations Recipes for War Rationed Cooking" published during WW II.

Brains

Court bouillon

VINAIGRETTE

½ pint oil or more if necessary

⅓ as much vinegar

Freshly ground pepper

A few capers

Onion, chopped

Parsley, chopped

Chervil

Tarragon

Chives

First carefully remove thin membrane which entirely covers brains. Try not to tear them as they are very delicate. Then soak brains in cold water with a little vinegar and salt to remove all blood. When they are white put them in boiling "court-bouillon" to cover; skim and simmer gently for ½ hour. The brains are then lifted out and ready to prepare in various ways.

Our favorite way is with sauce vinaigrette. Keep brains in large pieces, sauté gently in butter or margarine and serve with following sauce.

SAUCE VINAIGRETTE

To oil and vinegar add salt, freshly ground pepper, a few small capers, finely chopped onion, parsley, chervil, tarragon and chives. Stir well. This is very good with only onion, parsley and chives, if other herbs are not available.

COURT BOUILLON

Court bouillon is used for many things, especially fish, when a little vinegar is added to keep fish firm. It is simply salted water to which has been added minced carrots, onions, parsley and any herbs or seasonings you care for, such as bay leaf, thyme, celery and whole peppers. In some cases milk is added; sometimes wine; sometimes a slice of lemon.

Brains are delicious mixed with sweetbreads and mushrooms in a rich white sauce. Leftover chicken, hard-boiled eggs, gnocchi, asparagus tips, elbow macaroni or other things may be added to make this an ample and substantial dish.

Hans Kindler
First NSO Music Director
1931-1949

B's Secret Serbian Sarma

SERVES 8

1 head of cabbage with small veins, cored

1 large onion, grated

1 clove garlic, minced

1 pound ground chuck

½ pound ground pork

Paprika

Salt and pepper

6 tablespoons rice

2 eggs

1 small package sauerkraut

1 pound package of polksa kielbasa

Set aside a few raw outermost leaves of the cabbage to line the bottom of the cooking pot. Partially cook 6 tablespoons of rice and set aside.

Boil a large pot of water. Add 1 teaspoon salt. When water comes to a boil, add cabbage. With tongs, slowly loosen and separate each outer leaf from the cabbage. Each leaf should be pliable enough to roll, but not soft. Once many of the outer leaves are removed, set aside. Trim the large vines but do not cut through the leaf.

In a large bowl, mix the uncooked ground chuck, uncooked ground pork, eggs, grated onion, partially cooked rice, garlic, salt and pepper. Place 2 generous tablespoons of the uncooked blend into each cabbage leaf. Fold over one side on top of the meat then roll. Once you have rolled, tuck in the other end by continually poking your finger in until the other end is closed. If you cannot close the roll, you may use a toothpick. Take the raw leaves you have set aside and line the bottom of the cooking pot. Place half of the sauerkraut onto the raw leaves. Pile the rolls neatly on top of this.

Once all of the rolls are inside the pot, put the rest of the sauerkraut on top and sprinkle a layer of paprika on top of this. Pour 2 cups of water over the top and simmer for 1½ hours. After 1½ hours, add the kielbasa on top and simmer another half hour.

Sylvia Alimena
NSO Horn

Jessie's Barbequed Meatballs

SERVES 8

MEATBALLS

1 pound ground beef

1 egg, beaten

⅔ cup milk

1 teaspoon salt

Dash pepper

1 onion, minced

¼ teaspoon allspice

1 cup ground bread crumbs

Oil for frying

SAUCE

1 cup ketchup

½ cup chili sauce

1 tablespoon brown sugar

1 teaspoon salt

1 teaspoon chili powder

1 onion, grated

Preheat oven to 325 degrees. Mix all ingredients for the meatballs and form into small balls. Heat oil and brown in a frying pan. When browned place in a casserole dish.

Mix the ingredients for the sauce in a small bowl and pour over the browned meatballs. Bake covered one hour at 325 degrees.

Barbara A. Moore
NSO Women's Committee Member

LAMB

Roast Leg of Lamb

SERVES 6 TO 8

1 leg of lamb

2 cloves garlic

2 teaspoons salt

½ teaspoon pepper

1 teaspoon rosemary or thyme

¼ cup wine vinegar

2 tablespoons olive oil

1 onion, sliced

1 carrot, sliced

1½ cups apple juice

1-2 celery stalks

Preheat oven to 350 degrees. Trim excess fat from the leg of lamb. Score top fat in a diamond pattern. Crush garlic with seasonings, add vinegar and oil; rub over lamb. Place leg bone down in a roasting pan and place celery stalks on top of the lamb. Lower oven temperature to 325 degrees and roast for 1 hour.

Pour off excess fat and add onion and carrot slices. Pour the apple juice over the lamb. Finish roasting to medium rare about 155 degrees on a meat thermometer, or 25 minutes per pound, trimmed weight. Baste occasionally while roasting. Remove celery stalks when meat is finished.

Serve sauce with lamb.

Crystal L. Hundley-Evans
NSO National Trustee

Charcoal-Grilled Lamb with Sauce

Serves 8 to 10

6-pound leg of lamb, boned, fat removed and butterflied

1 cup olive or vegetable oil

⅔ cup lemon juice

3 cloves crushed garlic

2 bay leaves

6 sprigs parsley

2 teaspoons salt

½ teaspoon freshly ground pepper

1 tablespoon dried sage

1 tablespoon rosemary

1 tablespoon dried thyme

Sauce

½ cup beef stock

¼ cup red wine

2 tablespoons chopped shallots

3 tablespoons butter

3 tablespoons chopped parsley

Be sure all fat is removed from lamb.

Combine oil, lemon, garlic, bay leaves, parsley sprigs, salt, pepper and ½ teaspoon each sage, rosemary and thyme. Marinate meat in this mixture for 24 hours, turning occasionally.

Drain meat; reserve marinade. Sear each side of lamb on a hot grill; then cook 45 minutes to 1 hour, brushing with reserved marinade. Outside will be crusty and inside pink.

Sauce

Combine stock, wine, shallots and remaining spices. Boil rapidly and reduce to ½ cup. Remove from heat; add softened butter and chopped parsley. Pour over sliced meat.

Great with taboulleh.

Norma Dugger
Former NSO FANS Member

Hunan Lamb

SERVES 6 TO 8 AS PART OF A

MULTI-COURSE CHINESE DINNER

3-pound leg of lamb (weight includes bone)

½ cup peanut oil

12-16 dried hot red peppers

12 cloves garlic, peeled

1-inch cube ginger, sliced thin

2 scallions (including green portion) sliced in 1½-inch lengths

½ pound rock sugar*

2 teaspoons salt

2 tablespoons chili paste with garlic*

¼ cup dark soy sauce*

1¾ cups beer

* available in oriental groceries

Cut lamb into bite-size pieces. Boil enough water to cover meat; add lamb to boiling water and cook for 3 minutes, stirring occasionally. Drain; chill with cold water.

Heat peanut oil in wok. Add garlic and cook for 10 seconds. Add dried peppers and ginger; cook until peppers and garlic are dark brown. Add scallions and cook 20 to 30 seconds. Add lamb; cook (stirring) for 1 minute. Add rock sugar, chili paste, soy sauce and salt. Stir to blend and cook 1 minute.

Transfer to casserole and add beer. Cook for 45 minutes to 1 hour until meat is tender but not overcooked. Temperature for cooking should be medium heat to keep mixture below boiling point.

Henry Fogel
Former NSO Executive Director

Shish Kebab Marinated in Orange Juice

SERVES 4

1 pound lean lamb, cut into 1½-inch cubes

Onions, green peppers, tomatoes for skewering

MARINADE

¼ cup brown sugar

⅛ teaspoon ground cloves

¼ teaspoon dry mustard

⅓ cup chopped onion

Grated rind of ½ orange (about ½ tablespoon)

⅓ cup orange juice

¾ cup ketchup

1½ cups water

Combine all marinade ingredients in a saucepan. Bring to a boil and reduce heat. Simmer uncovered for about 30 minutes. Remove from heat and cool. Pour over lamb and marinate for at least 8 hours or overnight.

Skewer lamb cubes alternately with tomatoes, onions and green peppers. Baste periodically while broiling. Remaining marinade can be strained and used as a sauce for accompanying rice.

The lamb absorbs the orange flavor beautifully. Not good with beef.

Arthur Lieb

Kibbeh Bil Sineych (Baked Kibbi)

SERVES 6

2 cups fine Bulgur

2 pounds lean lamb, ground very fine

1 large onion, ground very fine

Salt and freshly ground pepper to taste

½ cup of water

FILLING

1 pound ground lamb

Salt, freshly ground pepper and allspice to taste

¼ -½ cup pine nuts

1¼ cups clarified butter

Rinse Bulgur in large amounts of water. Drain and squeeze out moisture handful by handful. Mix with ground meat and onion; grind together twice more. Add water as needed to mixture to make stiff paste.

Butter a flat 10x14-inch baking sheet. Spread half of kibbi on it. Brown rest of lamb in ¼ cup butter; add seasonings and pine nuts. Spread over kibbi. Cover with remaining kibbi. Score in squares or diamonds with a knife; loosen edges with a knife.

Pour rest of butter over top to cover it and bake in a 400 degree oven for 30 minutes or until golden brown. Serve hot or cold.

Embassy of Lebanon

Lamb Burgundy with Polenta

SERVES 6

4 tablespoons olive oil

4 pounds butterflied lamb leg, cubed

Salt and freshly ground pepper

Flour

1 large onion, finely chopped

5 garlic cloves, peeled and chopped

3 large carrots, peeled and finely chopped

1 cup tomato sauce

2½ cups burgundy wine

2 cups beef broth

2 bay leaves

2 teaspoons rosemary

1 cup polenta

½ cup grated Parmesan cheese

¼ cup butter

Over medium heat in a large dutch oven, heat olive oil. Season cubed lamb with salt and pepper and dredge in flour. In batches brown the cubed lamb. Remove to a plate.

Sauté the onion, garlic and carrots for about 10 minutes, until the onion is translucent.

Return the lamb to the dutch oven. Stir the tomato sauce, wine, broth, bay leaves and rosemary into the meat and vegetable mixture. Bring to a boil. Cover and simmer, stirring occasionally, for 1½ hours.

Uncover, increase heat to high and boil until the liquid thickens to sauce consistency. Salt and pepper to taste.

Prepare the polenta according to package directions. Add butter and Parmesan cheese to prepared polenta.

To serve, pass the polenta along with the lamb. The lamb is better if cooked a day before and reheated prior to serving.

Roberta A. Meredith
NSO Women's Committee Member

PORK

Cantonese Lettuce Burgers

SERVES 6 TO 8

1 pound lean, finely ground pork or chicken

1 small can baby peas

6 water chestnuts, chopped

1 head lettuce (iceberg, red or Romaine), well chilled

½ cup soy sauce

3 tablespoons sugar

2 teaspoons peanut oil

Fried rice

Chill wet lettuce for 5 minutes. Mix pork or chicken in marinade of soy sauce and sugar. In a frying pan or wok, heat the oil for 30 seconds. Cook pork or chicken mixture. Add peas and water chestnuts. Transfer to a warm baking dish.

Invite guests to serve themselves a lettuce leaf and spoon mixture into chilled lettuce leaves along with some fried rice. Then simply fold the leaf like a crêpe and eat with your fingers.

Leonard Slatkin
NSO Music Director
1996-Present

Mandarin Orange Pork Roast

SERVES 6

1 pork tenderloin, about 2 pounds

MARINADE
4 tablespoons brown sugar

½ teaspoon ground ginger

½ teaspoon ground cloves

1 teaspoon dry mustard

¼ cup ketchup

Juice from 1 11-ounce can mandarin oranges (in own juice)

Preheat oven to 350 degrees. Mix marinade. Pour into gallon size Ziploc bag. Add roast. Marinate for 2 hours, turning occasionally.

Place tenderloin in roasting pan and bake at 350 degrees for about 1 hour. Baste with marinade every 20 minutes; warm remaining marinade. Remove from oven, slice and top with remaining marinade.

Use the mandarin oranges as a garnish.

Marcia Farabee
NSO Principal Librarian

Stuffed Pork Loin with Bourbon

Serves 6 to 8

3-pound pork loin, boned

8-10 prunes

1 or more cups beef broth

¼ pound prosciutto or smoked ham, cut into thin slices

½ cup shelled pistachio nuts

½ cup Dijon mustard

⅔ cup brown sugar

2 tablespoons cooking oil

⅔ cup bourbon

Salt and freshly ground pepper to taste

Thyme, sage, and parsley to make bouquet garni

½ teaspoon arrowroot or cornstarch (optional)

Preheat oven to 375 degrees. Dry meat. Cut a deep pocket in pork from within 1 inch of either end of meat. Cut prosciutto or ham into strips.

Steep prunes in about 1 cup of beef broth. Remove prunes, but save liquid.

Insert prosciutto or ham strips, pistachios and prunes into pork pocket. Press meat back in place and tie securely. Paint meat with mustard; then roll in brown sugar.

Heat oil in a heavy, ovenproof cooking pot and brown meat in it, turning to brown evenly, for about 10 to 15 minutes. The sugar will caramelize, so be careful it does not burn.

Remove pot from burner. Pour half bourbon over meat and set aflame. When flame goes out, pour in remaining beef broth. Cover pot and set into a preheated 375 degree oven to cook for 1¾ hours.

Halfway through cooking, turn meat. Season with salt and pepper; add bouquet garni. Lower heat to 350 degrees. About 10 minutes before end of cooking time, add liquid saved from prunes.

This pork may be served hot or cold; best served cold only in summer. When pork is served hot, remove meat to a warm platter, strain cooking liquid and remove fat. Return liquid to pot and set over heat. Bring sauce to boil, adding remaining bourbon and stirring to dislodge sediments. Sauce may be thickened by bringing to a boil with arrowroot or cornstarch mixed with a little cold water. Taste and correct seasoning.

Whether pork is served cold or hot, slice it and lay it over a bed of watercress. If served hot, coat meat lightly with sauce and serve remaining sauce on the side.

Lonie Landfield

Pork Tenderloin Stuffed with Swiss Chard and Feta

SERVES 8

1 pound Swiss chard (red and green), stems discarded, coarsely chopped

6 large garlic cloves, thinly sliced

3 tablespoons olive oil

½ cup feta cheese, crumbled

3 pounds pork tenderloin (or boneless butterflied lamb leg)

1-2 tablespoons fresh rosemary (or dried)

1-2 tablespoons mixed Italian seasoning

1 large onion, coarsely chopped

1-2 leeks, sliced

1-2 cups dry red wine

1-2 cups beef broth

½ cup water

1 tablespoon cornstarch dissolved in cold water

Salt and pepper to taste

Peppercorns

Spool of white string

Preheat oven to 325 degrees. Wash Swiss chard and steam in the water clinging to the leaves, in a heavy covered skillet over medium heat for 3 to 5 minutes or until wilted. Drain, refresh under cold water and squeeze dry in kitchen towel. Add 2 tablespoons of olive oil to skillet and cook the garlic over moderate heat, stirring until golden brown. Transfer to a large bowl with a slotted spoon. Cook the onion and leek in the same way and add to the garlic. Add the chard, feta and herbs and mix thoroughly.

Pat the tenderloin dry and season with salt and pepper. Place 8 to 10 evenly spaced long strings crossways under the tenderloin (or under the two small tenderloins sitting side by side), and 1 to 2 strings lengthways. Spread the feta and chard mixture over the tenderloin, leaving a 1 inch border around the edges. Tie the crossways strings first, tying them very tightly to hold the meat together; then the two lengthways. You may need skewers as well.

Transfer the meat to a roasting pan and rub it with the remaining oil, rosemary, salt and pepper. Roast for 90 minutes or until the meat thermometer reads 140 degrees for medium rare. Transfer to chopping board and let stand for 20 minutes.

Skim fat from drippings; then deglaze the pan with the wine. Strain through a sieve into a saucepan and add the broth, some rosemary and water. Reduce to about 2 cups of liquid, stir in the cornstarch and simmer for several minutes until it thickens; then add peppercorns.

Jeannette Petite

VEAL

Sautéed Veal Scallops in Sour Cream Sauce

SERVES 2 TO 4

4 large veal scallops, sliced ⅜ inch thick and pounded to ¼ inch thickness

3 tablespoons unsalted butter

¼ cup finely chopped onion

3 tablespoons vegetable oil

SAUCE
Pan drippings and onions from skillet

2 tablespoons vermouth

1 cup sour cream

1 cup shredded goat cheese (Montrachet)

Salt and freshly ground pepper to taste

Heat 1 tablespoon butter and 1 tablespoon oil in a heavy skillet over moderate heat. When foam subsides, add onions and cook 3 to 5 minutes or until transparent. Scrape with spatula into a small bowl and set aside.

Add remaining butter and oil. When foam subsides, add veal and fry over moderate heat until golden brown (4 to 5 minutes each side). Remove to heated platter and warm in 220 degree oven while making sauce.

Return veal to skillet. Baste with sauce and let simmer for a few minutes. Serve at once.

SAUCE
Deglaze pan with 2 tablespoons vermouth. Add cooked onions. Cook over high heat, stirring constantly, 2 to 5 minutes. Reduce heat and stir in sour cream and cheese, a little at a time. Stir until melted and smooth, but do not boil. Add seasonings.

Leonard Slatkin
NSO Music Director
1996-Present

Escalope de Veau à la Moutarde

SERVES 3 TO 4

8 veal scallops

⅓ cup flour

Salt and freshly ground pepper

4 tablespoons butter

2 tablespoons minced shallots

¼ cup dry white wine

½ cup heavy cream

1 tablespoon Dijon mustard

Fresh chopped parsley

Place veal scallops on flat surface and pound thin. Blend flour with salt and pepper; coat scallops.

Heat butter in a large skillet until hot (not brown). Add scallops. Cook quickly until golden (about 2 minutes) and turn. Remove to warming dish; keep warm.

Add shallots to skillet and cook briefly, stirring. Add wine and cook, stirring, until nearly evaporated. Add cream and continue stirring as it comes to a boil. Cook about 30 seconds and then remove from heat. Stir in mustard. Do not cook further. Pour over scallops and serve. Sprinkle with parsley.

This sauce can also be made ahead, heated up and poured over baked chicken.

Paul R. Ignatius
Former NSO Board Member

Veal Birds in Tomato Sauce

SERVES 2 TO 4

4 veal scallops

4 prosciutto ham slices, thinly sliced

4-6 sage leaves

½ cup flour

¼ cup butter

Salt and freshly ground pepper

SAUCE

2 1-pound cans Italian plum tomatoes

2 teaspoons Italian seasoning

½ teaspoon basil

¼ cup butter

Salt and pepper veal scallops. On each piece of seasoned veal, place a similarly-sized slice of proscuitto and one sage leaf.

Roll up and tie with thread. Roll in flour; sauté in butter. Finish cooking in a well-seasoned tomato sauce for about 15 minutes.

SAUCE

Crush tomatoes in pan; add herbs and butter. Cook until some but not all liquid is reduced. Pour over veal birds and cook over low heat for 15 minutes.

Henryk Szeryng
Guest Artist, Violin

Super Scallopine

SERVES 4

8 veal scallops

1 avocado, sliced thin

2 fresh tomatoes, sliced

8 slices Jarlsberg or Swiss cheese

Lemon pepper and flour

3 tablespoons butter

Pound veal between sheets of wax paper. Sprinkle with lemon pepper and dredge with flour.

Melt butter in skillet and brown veal briefly. Cover veal with tomato slices and avocado slices. Top with cheese. Cover and cook over moderate heat for 5 minutes or until cheese is melted. Serve immediately.

Anne Watson
Former NSO FANS Member

Veal Basket Royal

MAKES 8 BASKETS

3 pounds veal, extra lean

1 bunch watercress, chopped

1 large shallot, chopped

1 cup Chablis wine

1 cup whipping cream

1 teaspoon butter

3 teaspoons flour

Salt and freshly ground pepper

3 cups oil

1 loaf solid white bread

For each basket, cut a 2x4-inch rectangular-shaped piece of solid white bread and fry in oil at 350 degrees or until light brown all around; set aside when done. When cool, remove center section to form a basket design.

Put soft butter into a bowl; add flour with a fork and mix together. It will become a sticky paste.

With a sharp knife, remove all remaining fat from veal and cut meat into strips. In a cooking pan, melt butter until brown and sauté veal a pound at a time. Set aside.

Sauté shallot and watercress together for 30 seconds. Pour in wine and let boil for 1 minute; then pour in whipping cream. When it starts to boil, add roux one teaspoon at a time and stir sauce until thick.

Put veal back into sauce and mix well for a couple of minutes. Place veal mixture into bread basket and serve.

Ridgewell's Caterer, Inc.

Osso Buco (Braised Veal Shanks)

Serves 8

8 veal shanks (2-2½ inches long)

1½ cups onions, finely chopped

½ cup carrots, finely chopped

½ cup celery, finely chopped

2 cloves garlic, finely chopped

4 tablespoons butter

Salt and freshly ground pepper

Flour

½ cup olive oil

1 cup dry white wine

1 teaspoon dried basil

½ teaspoon dried thyme

10 parsley sprigs

2 bay leaves

1 can chicken stock

3 cups whole canned tomatoes, drained, coarsely chopped

Preheat oven to 350 degrees. Securely tie each shank around the middle.

Melt the butter in a casserole over moderate heat. Add the onions, carrots, celery and garlic. Cook, stirring occasionally, until the vegetables are lightly colored. Remove from heat.

Season veal with salt and pepper. Roll them in flour and shake off excess. In a heavy 12-inch skillet, heat 6 tablespoons of the olive oil. Brown the veal over moderately high heat. Add more oil if necessary. Transfer browned pieces to the casserole on top of the vegetables.

Discard most of the fat from the skillet, leaving a film on the bottom. Pour in the wine and boil it briskly over high heat, reducing it to about ½ cup. Scrape bits clinging to pan. Stir in chicken stock, basil, thyme, tomatoes, parsley sprigs, bay leaves and bring to a boil. Pour mixture over veal. (If the liquid does not come halfway up the side of the veal, then add more stock.) Bring the casserole to a boil on top of the stove.

Cover and bake in the lower third of the oven, basting occasionally. In 1 hour and 15 to 30 minutes, the veal should be tender; test by piercing the meat with the tip of a sharp knife.

When transferring the shanks to a serving plate, remove the trussing strings.

Serve with Risotto alla Milanese.

—

Susan Porter
NSO Board Member

Marinated Sweetbreads

1½ pounds veal sweetbreads, cut into ½-inch cubes

2 tablespoons butter, clarified

Salt and freshly ground pepper

4 leaves fresh basil, chopped

1 teaspoon shallots, chopped

1 green onion, top only

1 tomato, peeled, seeded and diced

2 cloves garlic

2 tablespoons olive oil

1 teaspoon sherry vinegar

12 fava bean pods, shucked (Italian lima beans)

1 cup chicken stock

Cut sweetbreads into ½-inch cubes. Sauté in butter over high heat until cooked, approximately 3 minutes. Transfer sweetbreads to a plate and season to taste with salt and pepper.

Finely chop and add to sweetbreads basil, shallots, green onion and tomato, reserving 2 tablespoons of tomato for garnish.

Cut garlic cloves in half. Soak them in olive oil and sherry vinegar. Toss with above mixture and let marinate for 5 minutes.

Shuck fava beans and peel skin from each bean. Cook 4 minutes in chicken stock. Remove from stock and add to marinated sweetbreads. Toss, drain off marinade and set aside.

Arrange individual portions on 6 plates and drizzle each with 1 teaspoon of the marinade. Sprinkle with diced tomato.

Chef Yannick Cam
Le Pavillon Restaurant

The National Symphony Orchestra in the renovated Kennedy Center
Concert Hall with current Music Director Leonard Slatkin (2002).
Credit Donna Cantor McLean.

Note: *recipes marked with this icon are from the original National Symphony Orchestra*
Cookbook, published by FANS (Friends Assisting the National Symphony) in 1983.

PASTA & RICE

PASTA & RICE

Agnolotti alla Crema

SERVES 4

PASTA
¾ pound flour

3 eggs

Pinch salt

1 egg to brush dough

FILLING
4 ounces ricotta cheese

4 ounces mortadella

2 ounces spinach

SAUCE
6 ounces heavy cream

1½ ounces butter

1½ ounces Parmesan cheese

PASTA

Form mound of flour on a working surface. Break eggs into center and add a pinch of salt. Stir in flour. Gradually knead with your fingers and heel of your hand for at least 10 minutes, until dough is very elastic. Let rest for about 15 minutes wrapped in parchment.

Feed dough through a pasta machine several times until it becomes smooth and firm. Divide dough in half and roll out each piece in fairly thin sheets.

Place small mounds of filling on one sheet at regular intervals. Cover with second sheet of dough which has been brushed with beaten egg. Cut mounds with a round cutter. Gently lift each round with a spatula and place on a cookie sheet.

FILLING

Wash spinach well. Cook in boiling water until just tender; drain and let cool. Grind spinach, mortadella and ricotta cheese through a food mill and mix until smooth.

SAUCE

Place cream, butter and Parmesan cheese in a sauté pan and let simmer to a creamy consistency. In plenty of boiling, salted water, cook agnolotti until tender, yet firm. Drain and add to cream sauce. Serve immediately.

Chef Pierre Dupont
1789 Restaurant

Irena's Lasagne with Bolognese Sauce

SERVES 8 TO 10

2 pounds fresh flat sheets of pasta (green or yellow)

2 pounds fresh ricotta

2 pounds mozzarella, grated

2 cups freshly grated Parmesan cheese

½ cup (1 stick) unsalted butter

BOLOGNESE SAUCE

3 carrots, finely diced

3 onions, finely diced

3 celery stalks, finely diced

1 slice bacon, finely diced

3 tablespoons olive oil

¼ pound chicken liver, chopped

1 pound lean ground beef

1 pound lean ground veal or pork

1 cup dry red wine

2 teaspoons salt

Freshly ground pepper to taste

2 2-pound cans peeled plum tomatoes

4-ounce can tomato paste

½ cup water

Sauté carrots, onions, celery and bacon in large 4 to 6-quart enameled pot until onions are golden. Add chicken livers, beef and veal; brown. Break up any lumps in ground meat and then add wine. Cook until wine evaporates.

Add salt, pepper, tomatoes, tomato paste and water; bring to a boil. Cover and lower heat. Simmer 3 hours.

Preheat oven to 350 degrees.

Cut pasta into 10-inch lengths and cook in boiling salted water al dente, about 4 to 5 minutes. Drain and pat dry. Cook in batches.

Ladle a thin layer of Bolognese sauce into two, 9x12-inch ovenproof dishes. Layer with pasta, another layer of sauce, a layer of ricotta, ⅛ of mozzarella, and ⅛ of Parmesan. Continue these layers until ingredients are used up. (Don't worry if there are leftovers.) Finish with a layer of cheeses.

Dot with butter. Bake for ½ hour. Cool for 10 minutes before cutting.

Carol Becker
Former NSO FANS Member

Asparagus and Prosciutto Lasagne

SERVES 6

¼ pound fresh green pasta, whole flat sheets

¼ pound fresh regular pasta, whole flat sheets

½ cup Parmesan cheese, freshly grated

2 tablespoons butter

Salt and freshly ground pepper

SAUCE
1 onion, minced

1 garlic clove, minced

1 bay leaf

2 tablespoons olive oil

2 tablespoons butter

¼ pound thinly-sliced prosciutto or Westphalian ham, chopped

2 pounds asparagus, trimmed and sliced

1 cup dry white wine

1⅓ cups heavy cream

2 tablespoons flour

Cut tips off asparagus and reserve. Slice remaining stalks thinly on diagonal.

In a large, heavy skillet, sauté onion, garlic and bay leaf in oil and butter over moderate heat until onion is golden. Add prosciutto and cook for 1 minute, stirring. Add sliced asparagus stalks and cook, stirring again for 1 minute. Add wine and bring to a boil. Cover and simmer for 5 minutes. Uncover and cook over moderately high heat until wine is evaporated.

Mix cream with flour and stir into asparagus mixture. Again bring to boil, stirring. Simmer for 1 minute, season with salt and pepper and remove from heat. Discard bay leaf. Cut pasta into 10-inch lengths.

Cook pasta in boiling, salted water in batches for 3 minutes; it will not be very soft. Drain and cool in ice water; dry on paper towels.

Blanch asparagus tips, drain and cool under water. Pat dry.

Butter a 9x12-inch baking dish. Begin with a layer of yellow pasta, add one third of sauce and sprinkle with ⅓ cup Parmesan cheese. Add another layer, this time using green pasta, then half of remaining sauce. Again sprinkle ⅓ cup Parmesan. Add layer of yellow pasta, remaining sauce and ⅓ cup Parmesan.

Cover mixture with green pasta, scatter asparagus tips over top and sprinkle with remaining ½ cup Parmesan. Dot with butter and bake in a preheated 400 degree oven for 25 minutes, until golden and bubbly. Let rest for 5 minutes before serving.

Carol Becker
Former NSO FANS Member

Linguini Rosa

SERVES 8 AS A FIRST COURSE

2 pounds fresh tomato linguini

6 medium to large shallots, finely chopped

16-20 medium-size white mushrooms washed, peeled, finely sliced and rubbed with lemon juice, if not used immediately

2 cups heavy cream

6-8 tablespoons butter

1 cup Parmesan cheese

Freshly ground pepper

Salt

Use enamelled cast iron pot large enough to accommodate all cooked linguini. Sauté shallots to translucency and soften in a small portion of butter. Add mushrooms and sauté to desired doneness. Remove to a bowl with slotted spoon.

Put remaining butter and ⅔ of cream in saucepan, simmering over medium heat for at least a minute until thickened. Never boil cream.

Bring 6 quarts of water to a boil and add 2 tablespoons salt. Drop in linguini; cover when it returns to a boil. Pasta is cooked when returned to the boil. Drain immediately.

Return cooked, drained pasta to enamelled pan containing butter and cream. Place over low heat under linguini and toss with sauce. Add mushroom-shallot mixture, remaining cream and all cheese. Toss until well coated. Taste and correct seasoning. Serve immediately.

Mary S. Odyniec
Former NSO FANS Member

Spaghetti Puttanesca alla Moffo

SERVES 6

PASTA
3 cups flour

4 eggs

Pinch of salt

SAUCE
¼ pound butter

3 tablespoons olive oil

4 medium garlic cloves, finely chopped

20 pitted and halved olives

1 tablespoon capers

6 fresh cherry tomatoes or ½ can peeled tomatoes

2 teaspoons chopped parsley

8 anchovy filets

To make pasta, mound flour on kneading board. Make a hole in middle of flour; add eggs and salt. With a fork, gradually stir eggs beginning at center of mound and working out until all flour is mixed. Knead dough until it is smooth and firm and begins to blister on outside.

Cover dough with a mixing bowl and let rest for 1 hour. Cut 2-inch squares and press with roller until very fine. Allow to dry for about 10 minutes.

After all dough has been rolled out, flour kneading board. Fold rolled dough to 2 inches in diameter and then cut with a sharp, floured knife into ⅛-inch slices. After each piece is cut, open each piece of pasta and hang to dry fully.

SAUCE
Combine butter, oil, garlic and anchovies in saucepan over low heat. As soon as garlic begins to turn golden (about 30 seconds) add olives, capers and tomatoes. Stir another 30 seconds over high heat.

After sauce is made, boil pasta. The secret to making very good pasta is to be sure you have a large pot and a lot of water, much more than you think you need. As soon as pasta comes to top of water, is should be drained and put on a serving platter ready for the sauce.

Pour sauce over pasta and sprinkle with chopped parsley. Serve immediately.

A pinch of salt should be added to the water before pasta is put in, but in the case of Puttanesca, I do not put in salt because the anchovies are so salty.

Anna Moffo
Soprano, Guest Artist

Manicotti

SERVES 8 TO 10

SAUCE

¼ cup olive oil

1 cup finely chopped onion

1 clove garlic, crushed

1 can (2 pounds 3 ounces) Italian tomatoes, undrained

1 6-ounce can tomato paste

2 sprigs parsley

1½ cups water

1 tablespoon salt

2 teaspoons sugar

1 teaspoon dried oregano leaves

½ teaspoon dried basil

¼ teaspoon pepper

SHELLS

5 eggs

1¼ cups unsifted all-purpose flour

¼ teaspoon salt

1 teaspoon butter

FILLING

2 pounds ricotta cheese

1 package (8 ounces) mozzarella cheese, diced

⅓ cup grated Parmesan cheese

2 eggs

1 tablespoon chopped parsley

1 teaspoon salt

¼ teaspoon pepper

2 tablespoons grated Parmesan cheese

TO MAKE SAUCE

In hot oil in 6-quart kettle, sauté onion and garlic until golden brown – about 5 minutes. Add tomatoes, tomato paste, 1½ cups water, parsley sprigs, 1 tablespoon salt, sugar, oregano, basil, ¼ teaspoon pepper; mix well, mashing tomatoes.

Bring to boiling. Reduce heat and simmer in covered kettle for 1 hour while stirring occasionally.

TO MAKE SHELLS

In medium bowl, combine 5 eggs, the flour, ¼ teaspoon salt, and 1¼ cups water; with portable electric mixer, beat until smooth. Melt butter in 7-inch skillet. Pour in 2 tablespoons batter, rotating pan quickly to spread batter evenly over bottom of pan. Cook over medium heat, until top is dry and bottom is not brown. Turn out on wire rack to cool. Continue cooking batter, 2 tablespoons at a time, until all is used. As shells cool, stack them with wax paper between them.

Preheat oven to 350 degrees.

TO MAKE FILLING

In large bowl, combine ricotta, mozzarella, ⅓ cup Parmesan, 2 eggs, chopped parsley, 1 teaspoon salt, ¼ teaspoon pepper; beat with wooden spoon until well blended. Place about ¼

continued...

cup filling in center of each shell and roll up. Spoon some of the tomato sauce in bottom of two greased 13x9x2-inch baking dishes. Place shells, seam side, in single layer in dishes. Cover with remaining tomato sauce; sprinkle with 2 tablespoons Parmesan cheese. Bake uncovered for 30 minutes or until bubbly. Freezes well.

Cookbook Committee

Baked Ziti

SERVES 8

1 16-ounce package ziti (or penne) pasta

1 15-ounce package ricotta cheese

1 16-ounce package shredded mozzarella cheese

1 egg, lightly beaten

¼ cup chopped fresh parsley

1 clove garlic, crushed

¼ teaspoon pepper

¼ cup grated Parmesan cheese

Cook pasta following package directions; drain. Grease a 2 quart casserole dish. In large bowl, blend ricotta cheese, 1 cup mozzarella cheese, egg, parsley, garlic and pepper. Stir in ziti. Transfer to casserole, and sprinkle top with remaining mozzarella and Parmesan cheese. Bake in 350 degree oven until top is golden, approximately 30 minutes.

Mary Rita Rossetti

Fettuccine Alfredo

SERVES 4 TO 6

1 pound fettuccine

2 cups heavy cream, room temperature

4 ounces (8 tablespoons) unsalted butter

Salt and freshly ground white pepper to taste

1 cup Parmesan cheese, freshly grated (preferably the Parmigiano-Reggiano brand)

Put a large pot of water on to boil. Add salt.

In a large sautéuse or skillet put 1½ cups of heavy cream and all of the butter. Place pan over moderate heat and slowly melt the cream and butter together. Simmer. Season the sauce.

Cook the pasta, drain it and quickly add to the cream sauce. Pour in the remaining ½ cup of cream and add the grated cheese. Toss.

Cookbook Committee

Fettuccine Fredde alla Pronto

SERVES 4

6 tablespoons olive oil

2 cloves garlic, finely minced

2 ounces pignoli nuts (pine nuts)

1 cup tomatoes, skinned, seeded and roughly chopped

1 pound fresh fettuccine

1 cup Italian-style tuna, cut into rough pieces

½ red pimento, cut into thin strips

6 black olives, pitted and roughly chopped

1-2 tablespoons chopped parsley

2 tablespoons red wine vinegar

Salt and pepper to taste

Additional parsley for garnish

Heat olive oil in a skillet, add the garlic and pignoli nuts. Sauté over low heat 5 minutes or until garlic turns translucent and pine nuts are golden. Add tomatoes and cook one minute. Turn mixture into a large bowl. Cool.

Cook fettuccine in a large pot of rapidly boiling, lightly salted water until firm to the bite. When pasta is "al dente" stop boiling by adding a glass of cold water. Drain.

Add the cooked pasta to the large bowl containing the oil-garlic-pignoli nut mixture and toss gently to coat. Add the tuna, pimento, olives, parsley and red wine vinegar. Turn with two large spoons to blend. Season with salt and freshly ground pepper. Sprinkle remaining parsley on top and serve at room temperature.

Susan Porter
NSO Board Member

Tomato Angel Hair Pasta with Basil and Crab

SERVES 4

1½ cups butter

4 teaspoons chopped, fresh shallots

4 teaspoons chopped, fresh basil

4 teaspoons chopped, fresh parsley

6 cups fresh, peeled tomatoes

1 pound fresh, backfin crabmeat

1¼ pounds fresh angel hair pasta

Melt butter in saucepan. Add shallots, basil, parsley and tomatoes. Bring to a boil. Add crabmeat.

Douse pasta in boiling water for 90 seconds. Drain and add to hot sauce. Serve at once.

Chef Monroe Duncan
Suddenly Last Summer Restaurant
Norfolk, Virginia

Scapinash con Burro Nocciola, Salvia e Parmigiano

SERVES 4

8 sheets of fresh egg pasta (6 x 8 inches)

½ cup Parmesan cheese, grated

3 ounces butter

1 cup fresh ricotta cheese

2 ounces dry, aged ricotta cheese, grated

1 tablespoon golden raisins, soaked and chopped (soak in warm water until soft, drain)

2 Amaretto cookies, crumbled

3 ounces 1-day-old country bread, diced and soaked with milk, then squeezed to remove the excess moisture

1 egg

1 tablespoon chopped chives, parsley or basil

1 pinch nutmeg

Fresh sage

Salt and pepper to taste

In a sauté pan, place 1 ounce of butter and dry ricotta cheese and sauté until golden. Allow to cool. Combine fresh and dry ricottas, chives, ½ of the Parmesan cheese, raisins, Amaretto cookies, bread, egg, pinch of nutmeg and season to taste. Mix together very well.

With the help of a pastry bag, place a dollop of ricotta filling on top of a sheet of pasta brushed with egg wash, at one inch intervals. Close the ravioli, placing another sheet of pasta on top and sealing all around each ravioli. Pushing the excess air out, cut symmetrically with a ravioli wheel.

Cook in boiling, salted water for 4 minutes. Add oil to the boiling water so that the raviolis do not stick together. In the meantime, brown the butter and sage in a saucepan. When it has a nice hazelnut color, add the drained raviolis and Parmesan cheese.

Chef Cesare Lanfranconi
Tosca Restaurant

Spaghetti Pie

SERVES 6

8 ounces spaghetti

2 tablespoons butter

⅓ cup Parmesan cheese, grated

2 well-beaten eggs

1 pound ground beef

½ cup chopped onion

1 8-ounce can crushed tomatoes

1 3-ounce can tomato paste

1 teaspoon sugar

1 clove garlic, crushed

1 cup ricotta cheese

½ cup shredded mozzarella cheese

Cook and drain spaghetti. Add butter, eggs and Parmesan cheese using a fork. Form into a "crust" in a 10-inch buttered pie plate.

Preheat oven to 325 degrees. Brown ground beef. Add onion, garlic, sugar and both types of tomatoes and heat through. Spread ricotta over center of crust. Top with sauce. Bake at 325 degrees for 10 minutes. Add mozzarella cheese and continue baking for another 10 minutes. Let cool for 10 minutes before cutting.

Marcia Farabee
NSO Principal Librarian

Trioletta (Pineapple, Cheese, Noodle Squares)

MAKES APPROXIMATELY 30 SQUARES

8 ounces fine egg noodles

¼ pound butter

5 eggs, beaten

2 pounds cottage cheese (large curd)

12-ounce can crushed pineapple, drained

1 pint sour cream

¾ cup sugar

½ teaspoon salt

1 teaspoon vanilla

Cook noodles according to directions and drain. Melt butter. Pour half into baking dish. Put noodles into mixing bowl. Add remaining butter, drained pineapple, salt and vanilla; mix well. Fold sour cream into beaten eggs and add to mixture. Finally, add cottage cheese and sugar, stirring gently until blended.

Pour into a 10x13x2-inch baking dish over melted butter. Bake at 425 degrees for 45 minutes or until top and sides are light brown. Let cool and cut into 2½-inch squares. Can be served hot or cold.

Samuel Levy
Former NSO Violin

July 4th Pasta Salad

SERVES 8 TO 10

1 pound rotelle, twists or fettuccine

1 bunch parsley, chopped

6-ounce can small pitted black olives, drained

2 4½-ounce cans chopped black olives

8-ounce can artichoke hearts, or more, drained and cut in quarters

1 bunch scallions, chopped

1 green pepper, chopped fine

1½ cups dressing

3-5 pieces cooked chicken, diced

¼ pound sliced salami, chopped

DRESSING

½ cup fresh lemon juice

¾ cup olive oil

¼ cup mayonnaise

½ teaspoon seasoned salt

Freshly ground pepper

Cook pasta until al dente. Drain and put in large bowl.

While pasta is still warm, add remaining ingredients and dressing. Toss well.

Refrigerate at least 4 hours, tossing occasionally. Serve with sliced tomatoes sprinkled with fresh basil, olive oil, vinegar and salt.

If to be used at a picnic or when refrigeration is unavailable, mayonnaise can be omitted.

Joan C-C Oppenheimer

Carol Mason's Pasta Salad

SERVES 8

1 cup small tomato pasta shells

1 cup small spinach pasta shells

2 teaspoons salt

2 cups cubed zucchini

⅓ cup vinegar

1 teaspoon prepared mustard

1 small clove garlic, crushed

1 tablespoon Worcestershire sauce

1 cup vegetable oil

Pinch freshly ground pepper

1 cup Genovesi dried tomatoes, drained and cut into strips

8 ounces feta cheese or goat cheese, cubed

TO SERVE

1 pound fresh spinach leaves, washed and dried

2 tablespoons chopped fresh parsley

2 tablespoons chopped fresh cilantro leaves

Cook tomato and spinach pasta in a large pot of boiling water seasoned with ½ teaspoon salt until tender, 8 to 10 minutes. Rinse, drain and set aside. Blanch zucchini in boiling water seasoned with ½ teaspoon salt until crisp-tender, 2 to 4 minutes. Rinse in cold water, drain and set aside.

In a small mixing bowl, combine remaining teaspoon salt, vinegar, mustard, garlic, Worcestershire sauce and oil; season with pepper and beat with a wire whisk until mustard is incorporated. Taste and correct seasoning if necessary.

In a large mixing bowl, combine cooked pasta with 1 cup of the vinaigrette and toss. Allow pasta to rest and absorb the vinaigrette for about 30 minutes.

Just before serving time, add remaining vinaigrette, zucchini, tomatoes and cheese and toss well. Taste and correct seasoning again if necessary.

To serve, arrange a bed of fresh spinach leaves on individual serving plates, pile pasta salad on top and garnish with chopped parsley and cilantro.

Carol Mason

Summer Pasta

SERVES 4

5-6 fresh tomatoes, peeled and cut into ½-inch cubes

1 ball fresh mozzarella cheese cut into ½-inch cubes

Fresh basil, minced

¼ cup olive oil

Fettuccini egg noodles, homemade preferred

Salt and freshly ground pepper to taste

Parmesan cheese

In a large pasta bowl mix together tomatoes, mozzarella cheese, basil, olive oil, salt and pepper. Prepare pasta and drain completely. Do not rinse in cold water, as pasta should be hot.

Immediately place pasta in pasta bowl and combine with tomatoes and cheese mixture. Thoroughly toss together and add Parmesan cheese to taste. Serve at room temperature.

Itzhak Perlman
Guest Conductor and Violinist

Beautiful Baked Rice

SERVES 8

5 tablespoons butter

2 cups rice

¼ cup onion, minced

½ teaspoon garlic, minced

3 cups chicken broth

3 sprigs parsley

2 sprigs thyme or ½ teaspoon, dried

1 bay leaf

Pinch cayenne or Tabasco

Melt 2 tablespoons butter in heavy saucepan or ovenproof dish. Sauté onions and garlic, stirring with a wooden spoon, until onion is clear.

Add rice and stir briefly over low heat until well coated with butter. Stir in stock, making sure there are no lumps in rice. Add remaining seasonings.

Cover with tight-fitting lid, and place in 400 degree oven. Bake 20 to 25 minutes. Remove cover and discard parsley and thyme. Using a 2-prong fork, stir in remaining butter. Rice can be made up to 2 days ahead and reheated very slowly in a 200 degree oven for 1 hour.

Mrs. Kenneth Gaarder

Lobster Risotto

SERVES 6

¾ pound pre-boiled lobster meat (found in fish market or gourmet stores)

10 ounces of Arborio rice (Carnaroli rice preferred)

Quarter of a gallon of lobster stock (found in gourmet stores)

3 ounces of butter

2 ounces of roasted tomatoes

½ cup tomato sauce

10 pieces of basil leaves, finely cut

2 tablespoons white truffle oil

½ onion, chopped

1 tablespoon garlic olive oil

½ cup white wine

1 tablespoon Italian parsley

Salt and pepper

To begin, cut the lobster meat into cubes. Mix the garlic olive oil with the onion in cooking pan for one minute on medium to high heat. Continually stir throughout the whole process. Add rice and let cook for a few minutes. Add white wine and continue stirring.

When white wine is evaporated, begin to add in little amounts lobster stock, until the stock has covered the rice. Stir constantly. Make sure the mixture is always boiling. Add the lobster stock for 10 minutes, very slowly.

Begin to add the roasted tomato, the tomato sauce, basil leaves and lobster meat (already cut in cubes). Let the mixture cook for another few minutes. Add butter, Italian parsley, white truffle oil, salt and pepper to taste.

Chef Fabrizio Aielli
Teatro Goldoni Restaurant

Risotto alla Milanese

SERVES 8

3 cans chicken broth mixed with 3 cups of water

1 small yellow onion, finely chopped

2 tablespoons vegetable oil

5 tablespoons butter

2 cups Arborio rice

½ teaspoon saffron

½ cup freshly grated Parmigiano-Reggiano cheese

Salt and freshly ground pepper, as needed

Bring the broth to a gentle boil and let simmer slowly. Add the saffron.

In a heavy-bottomed skillet, heat 3 tablespoons of butter and the oil. Add the onions and cook until translucent. Sauté the rice and stir until it is coated.

Using a ladle, add simmering broth to the rice, one ladleful at a time. When rice dries out, add another ladleful. Continue to stir. You cannot stop this process until all the liquid is absorbed.

Risotto is done when it is firm (al dente), not mushy. This process takes 20 to 30 minutes. Five minutes before rice is finished, add Parmigiano cheese and remaining 2 tablespoons of butter. Stir. Salt and pepper to taste.

Susan Porter
NSO Board Member

Shahjanhani Biryani (Spiced Saffron Rice)

SERVES 8

½ cup plus 2 tablespoons butter

1 whole chicken breast, skinned, boned and cut into bite-size pieces

4 medium onions, minced

1 tablespoon ginger, minced

2 garlic cloves, minced

16 whole cloves

4 4-inch cinnamon sticks

2 teaspoons turmeric

2 teaspoons cumin seeds

1½ teaspoons ground nutmeg

1½ teaspoons ground mace

¾ teaspoon cardamom seeds

¾ teaspoon cayenne

2 cups uncooked, converted rice

4 cups chicken stock or broth

2 teaspoons salt

1 teaspoon sugar

1½ teaspoons saffron threads

2 medium onions, cut lengthwise into thin strips

¾ cup dark raisins, plumped in water

¼ cup light raisins, plumped in water

½ cup unsalted cashews, sautéed in butter

½ cup shelled pistachios

½ cup slivered almonds, sautéed in butter

Silver leaf, optional (available at Indian grocery)

Melt 2 tablespoons butter in a 6-quart pan. Sauté chicken over medium heat until golden. Remove and set aside.

In same pan melt ½ cup butter. Add minced onion and cook until soft. Stir in ginger and garlic; sauté briefly.

Stir in cloves, cinnamon sticks, turmeric, cumin seeds, nutmeg, mace, cardamom seeds and cayenne. Add ½ cup butter. When melted, mix in rice and cook over medium heat until golden, stirring frequently. Stir in stock, salt, sugar and saffron threads. Return chicken to pan. Bring to boil, cover and cook over low heat for 45 to 50 minutes, until liquid has been absorbed.

Melt ¼ cup butter in medium skillet. Cook onion strips until well browned. Drain on paper towels.

Arrange rice on platter. Layer in following order: dark raisins, light raisins, cashews, pistachios, almonds, onions and if desired, silver leaf.

Mrs. Zubin Mehta
Wife of Guest Conductor, Zubin Mehta

Couscous with Onions and Raisins

SERVES 6

3 pounds meat, cut into pieces

9 ounces chick peas, soaked overnight

1 onion, sliced

½ teaspoon saffron

1 teaspoon pepper

½ teaspoon salt

5 pints water

3 cups couscous

2 pounds raisins

2 pounds onions, finely sliced

4 ounces butter

Put the meat, chick peas, sliced onion and spices in the bottom of a steamer with the water. Cook over medium heat for about an hour. Meanwhile, put the couscous in a colander (use cheesecloth on the bottom if holes are too large) and rinse under cold water. Drain for about 20 minutes. Put colander on top of main pot to steam for 15 minutes.

Remove colander from heat and place couscous on a large dish. Then add raisins and finely sliced onions. Little by little mix them into the couscous with your hands or a fork. It must not be lumpy. Separate the grains. Put the couscous back in the colander, on top of the steaming pot for another 15 to 20 minutes. Total steaming time should be 30 minutes or more. Cooking time will depend on when the meat is cooked. The sauce should not be too thin.

Replace couscous on large dish, add butter and mix well.

Serving suggestion: Place a "dome" of couscous in the center of a large dish, place the meat on top and pour enough broth over all, little by little.

Laila Benaissa
Embassy of Morocco

Violinist Glenn Donnellan and Assistant Principal Bass Richard Barber
with a young student at the East Nashville Center for the Creative Arts
on the NSO's Tennessee Residency (2004). Credit Scott Suchman.

Note: *recipes marked with this icon are from the original National Symphony Orchestra*
Cookbook, published by FANS (Friends Assisting the National Symphony) in 1983.

VEGETABLES

VEGETABLES

David's Roasted Vegetables

SERVES 8 TO 10

¾ cup balsamic vinegar

½ cup olive oil

2 cloves garlic, finely chopped

Dried and/or fresh thyme, oregano, basil, rosemary to taste

Salt and ground pepper to taste

1 medium eggplant

2-4 zucchini (depending on size)

Variety of fresh peppers (green, red, yellow, orange)

2 cups whole mushrooms

2 sweet onions

3 medium tomatoes

4 ounces chevre

6 ounces Kalamata olives or to taste

Prepare vinaigrette using vinegar, olive oil, garlic, herbs, salt and pepper. Slice eggplant, zucchini, peppers, onions and tomatoes to ½-inch thick. Marinate with whole mushrooms in vinaigrette for 10 minutes.

Layout vegetables evenly on 2 cookie sheets lined with foil, and sprayed with non-stick cooking spray. Roast at 450 degrees for 25 to 30 minutes, turning every five minutes.

Allow to cool slightly. Then mix in chevre, olives and drizzle with olive oil, salt and pepper to taste. Serve warm or chilled.

Use other vegetables or vary according to the season.

Jennifer Leed
NSO Administrative Staff Member

Stuffed Summer Squash

SERVES 4

5 yellow squash, use medium-large size if used as main course or use smaller squash if used for side dish

4 hard boiled eggs, chopped

1 large onion

1 large garlic clove

Bread crumbs, preferably Italian seasoned

Olive oil

Salt and freshly ground pepper to taste

Parsley

Stewed tomatoes, fresh or canned

Cut summer squash lengthwise, scoop out seeds carefully and discard. Parboil squash in salted, boiling water until just tender. Cut off neck from 8 halves and set aside. You will now have 8 squash "boats."

Coarsely chop necks and extra halves. Set aside. Chop onion and garlic. Sauté onion, garlic and chopped squash in olive oil until onion is transparent. Remove from heat and put entire contents into large bowl. Add chopped eggs, chopped parsley and enough bread crumbs to hold mixture together. Add a bit more oil if necessary. Season to taste. Stuff squash boats with mixture.

Place a layer of the stewed tomatoes in shallow pan or oven-proof dish. Place stuffed squash on top. The boats should fit snugly into pan. Do not use too large a pan or the boats will spread and possibly split. Add more tomatoes if desired. Bread crumbs can be sprinkled lightly on tops of boats, if desired.

Bake uncovered for approximately 30 to 45 minutes or until thoroughly heated. Serve with additional stewed tomatoes, if desired.

Variation: Brown Italian sausage (removed from casing) with onion and garlic. Use just the necks of the squash, but not more. Add bread crumbs, salt and pepper to taste and stuff boats with mixture.

Virginia C. Mars
NSO Board Member

Creamed Leeks

SERVES 6

2 bunches leeks

1 cup heavy cream

1 ounce water

2 tablespoons butter

Salt and freshly ground pepper to taste

Clean leeks (soak in water and separate to get all sand out). Dice into ¼-inch pieces. Use all of white and only light green part of stalks.

Place water and butter in a pan large enough to hold leeks. Add leeks and cook over medium heat for 20 to 25 minutes. Be careful it does not burn or stick. Stir occasionally. Season with salt and pepper.

When leeks are tender, add heavy cream and reduce cream until consistency is thick. Correct seasonings.

Cookbook Committee

Stuffed Eggplant Casserole

SERVES 4

1 large eggplant

1 cup chopped onion

1 cup chopped fresh mushrooms

1¼ teaspoons sweet basil or oregano

1 teaspoon salt

¼ teaspoon freshly ground black pepper

2 tablespoons butter

1 cup cooked ground beef

½ cup dry bread crumbs

Preheat oven to 350 degrees.

Wash eggplant, wrap it in aluminum foil and bake for 50 minutes, or until partly done. Cut in half; remove pulp to within ½ inch of outer skin. Chop pulp.

Sauté onions, mushrooms and seasonings in butter and add to eggplant pulp. Add meat and bread crumbs; mix well. Spoon mixture into eggplant shells and fit them into a casserole.

Bake long enough to heat them, 15 to 20 minutes. Garnish with parsley or grated Parmesan cheese.

Leontyne Price
Soprano, Guest Artist

Stuffed Aubergines

SERVES 8

4 medium eggplants

2 onions, finely chopped

2 cloves crushed garlic

4-6 ounces thinly-sliced, fresh mushrooms

4 large ripe, red tomatoes, skinned, seeded and chopped

1 tablespoon tomato purée

Pitted black olives

3 ounces browned bread crumbs

3 ounces grated Gruyère cheese

½ pint stock (beef or chicken)

5-6 chopped anchovy filets

2 tablespoons chopped parsley

Marjoram, thyme and oregano

Cut eggplants in half, lengthwise; scoop out pulp, leaving shells intact. Salt and drain shells for about 30 minutes; then rinse and dry carefully.

Fry onions, eggplant pulp and mushrooms gently in some butter until very soft. Add fresh tomatoes, tomato purée, herbs, garlic and stock, stirring well. Add anchovies and olives. Cook briefly.

Mix bread crumbs, cheese and parsley and add cooked tomato mixture.

Rub skin of each halved eggplant shell with olive oil and pile mixture into each half.

Bake in a covered dish in a moderate 350 degree oven until shells have softened and are cooked through.

Yehudi Menuhin
Guest Conductor and Guest Violinist

Broccoli Soufflé

SERVES 4 TO 6

3 cups broccoli

8 ounces sour cream

½ cup grated Parmesan cheese

6 tablespoons butter

4 egg yolks

5 egg whites

2 tablespoons chopped onion

½ teaspoon freshly ground pepper

1 teaspoon lemon juice

Dash salt

Peel and trim broccoli. Drop in boiling water for 2 minutes. Drain and pat dry. Place broccoli and all ingredients except egg whites in a food processor fitted with steel blade. Process, scraping sides once or twice for 2 minutes or until puréed. This can be done ahead and stored in refrigerator.

Whip egg whites until stiff and fold into purée. Pour into buttered baking dish that has been dusted with Parmesan cheese.

Bake in preheated 375 degree oven turned down to 350 degrees and bake for 30 to 40 minutes.

Pam Kloman
Former NSO FANS Member

Carrot Soufflé

SERVES 4

1 pound carrots

3 eggs

½ cup sugar; less if carrots are sweet

3 tablespoons flour

1 teaspoon baking powder

1 teaspoon vanilla

¼ pound (1 stick) butter

Dash of cinnamon

Dash of nutmeg

TOPPING

¼ cup crushed corn flakes or bread crumbs

2 tablespoons brown sugar

2 tablespoons butter

Dash cinnamon and nutmeg

¼ cup chopped walnuts, optional

Cut up carrots. Cook well. Strain and purée them in a food processor. Cool carrots. Add 3 eggs to purée. Blend in sugar, flour, baking powder, vanilla, butter and seasonings.

Grease an oven-proof casserole dish. Preheat oven to 350 degrees. Mix topping and put on top of carrot mixture.

Bake uncovered for 1 hour and serve hot.

Cookbook Committee

Favorite Brussels Sprouts

SERVES 6

2 pounds small Brussels sprouts

½ cup shelled peanuts, in halves or very coarsely chopped

2 tablespoons butter

2 tablespoons peanut oil

1 tablespoon lemon juice

1 teaspoon sugar

1 teaspoon salt

Bring a large pot of salted water to a boil. Meanwhile, cut a deep X in the stem end of each Brussels sprout to ensure even cooking. Prepare a medium bowl of ice water. Add the sprouts to the boiling water; parboil with lid off until almost tender, about 7 minutes; drain. Immediately plunge drained sprouts into ice water to set their bright green color and to stop the cooking. Drain.

Dissolve sugar in lemon juice. In a sauté pan, gently toast peanuts in oil until evenly light brown. Add butter and lemon juice mixture to pan, then the reserved Brussels sprouts. Salt to taste. Cook on medium heat just long enough to heat through.

Emil de Cou
NSO Associate Conductor

Smothered Cabbage

SERVES 4 TO 6

Having always resented overcooked vegetables, I prize this quick method of preparing cabbage for its flavor and convenience.

1 small, tight head cabbage

2 shredded lettuce leaves

1 small Bermuda onion, sliced

Pinch of sugar

Vegetable oil for frying

Caraway seeds, optional

Salt and freshly ground pepper to taste

Shred cabbage, as you would cole slaw; rinse it in lukewarm water first, then in cold water to crisp it.

Heat vegetable oil briefly over moderate heat in a heavy frying pan. Add shredded cabbage, salt and pepper to taste. Cover tightly for about 2 minutes; toss cabbage briefly. Add lettuce leaves to provide moisture for steaming and a few thinly-sliced rounds of onion. Cover tightly again and let cook for another 3 minutes.

Remove cover and sprinkle a pinch of sugar on cabbage; add caraway seeds, if desired, and toss cabbage briefly. Serve immediately.

Calvin B. LeCompte, Jr.

Vegetable Mousse

SERVES 4 TO 6

1 pound carrots, cut in chunks

1 package frozen artichoke hearts

2 tablespoons butter

1 package frozen, chopped spinach, defrosted and squeezed dry

1 medium onion, chopped fine

3 tablespoons chopped, fresh dill or 1½ tablespoons dried dill

5 large eggs

1 cup heavy cream

½ cup Parmesan cheese

½ cup milk

Salt and freshly ground pepper

Nutmeg to taste

Thoroughly grease sides and bottom of a loaf pan. Line with wax paper and grease again. Set aside.

Cook or steam carrots in small amount of water and drain. Cook artichoke hearts and drain.

Melt butter in medium-size pan and add spinach, onion and dill. Sauté over medium heat until onion is tender and spinach is dry.

Combine eggs, cream, milk, cheese, salt, pepper and nutmeg and blend until smooth.

In a food processor, combine a third of egg mixture with each of above vegetables. Process each briefly until blended. Arrange in layers, spreading each out evenly. Put artichokes on bottom, followed by carrots and then spinach.

Cook in a bain-marie (sit loaf pan in a larger pan filled with water a third up sides of loaf pan) for 1¼ hours in a 375 degree oven. Remove from oven and let stand for 10 minutes. Invert onto serving dish. Remove wax paper. Let stand 20 minutes before serving or refrigerate and serve very cold.

Howard de Franceaux

Spinach Casserole

SERVES 4

2 10-ounce packages frozen spinach

6 ounces cream cheese, softened

¼ pound butter, melted and seasoned with salt and freshly ground pepper

¼ cup bread crumbs (half plain and half seasoned)

¾ teaspoon sage

Cook and drain spinach well. Mix softened cream cheese with half of butter and add to spinach.

Grease a 9-inch Pyrex pie plate or small shallow casserole. Pour in spinach mixture. Add remaining butter to bread crumbs and sage. Spread over top of spinach.

Bake at 350 degrees for 30 minutes.

Cookbook Committee

Corn Spoonbread

SERVES 8

1 8-ounce package cornbread mix

2 eggs, beaten

1 stick butter, melted

8 ounces sour cream

1 8-ounce can kernel corn, drained

1 8-ounce can creamed corn

¼ cup Swiss cheese, grated

Combine all ingredients except cheese and put in greased 2-quart casserole dish. Place in preheated 350 degree oven and bake for 30 minutes. Sprinkle grated Swiss cheese on top and bake an additional 10 minutes, or until the cheese is melted and bubbly. Serve warm.

Variation: Substitute ½ cup grated Gruyère cheese for ¼ cup grated Swiss cheese

Christopher Wolf
NSO Board Member

Corn Soufflé

SERVES 8 TO 10

24-ounce bag of frozen yellow corn, slightly thawed

1 pint of whipping cream

6 eggs

3 tablespoons sugar

Dash of salt

¼ cup butter

Whip the eggs until well beaten using an electric mixer. Add in whipping cream, sugar and salt. Gradually fold in yellow corn. Pour mixture into greased 9x13-inch casserole serving dish. Put pats of butter on top. Bake at 325 degrees for 50 minutes to 1 hour. Should be slightly browned.

Anna Pfeiffer
NSO Board Member

Sweet Potato Casserole

SERVES 6 TO 8

3 cups mashed, cooked sweet potatoes

½ cup granulated sugar

½ teaspoon salt

2 eggs

⅓ stick butter

½ cup milk

1 teaspoon vanilla

TOPPING
1 cup brown sugar

1 cup chopped nuts

⅓ cup flour

⅓ stick melted butter

Mix together sweet potatoes, sugar, salt, eggs and butter. Add milk and vanilla last.

Pour into a greased baking dish. Sprinkle topping over sweet potato mixture and bake at 350 degrees for 30 to 35 minutes.

Edna E. Powers
Former NSO FANS Member

Sweet Potato Soufflé

SERVES 8

2½ cups cooked, mashed sweet potatoes

1 cup sugar

¼ cup butter or margarine

2 eggs, beaten

¼ cup evaporated milk

2 teaspoons vanilla

Dash of salt

TOPPING

1 small can crushed pineapple

½ cup sugar

¼ cup flour

¼ cup butter

1 egg, beaten

Preheat oven to 375 degrees. Mix together mashed sweet potatoes, 1 cup sugar, ¼ cup butter or margarine, 2 eggs, evaporated milk, vanilla and salt and place in baking dish.

To prepare topping, mix together crushed pineapple, ½ cup sugar, flour, ¼ cup butter and 1 egg and spread evenly over the top of the sweet potatoes mixture. Be certain to allow at least ¼ of an inch at the top of the dish for the soufflé will rise slightly while baking.

Bake sweet potato soufflé for 30 to 40 minutes in a 375 degree oven.

Crystal L. Hundley-Evans
NSO National Trustee

Potatoes Supreme

SERVES 6

🎵

Great on a buffet table!

2 cups potatoes

1 pound onions

¼ pound bacon

Salt and freshly ground pepper to taste

2 cups dry white wine

2 cups sour cream

½ pound grated Swiss cheese

1½ tablespoons butter

Peel potatoes. Cut potatoes, onions and bacon into cubes. Place in buttered casserole. Salt and pepper to taste. Mix well. Pour wine over potatoes. Cook uncovered at 325 degrees for 1 hour and 15 minutes. Do not allow to get mushy.

Add butter, Swiss cheese and sour cream. Blend carefully until cheese is melted. Adjust seasonings. Return to oven at 300 degrees. Bake until bubbly, about 25 minutes.

Marty Platt

Twice Baked Potatoes Cottage Style

SERVES 4

2 medium baking potatoes

½ cup low-fat cottage cheese

¼ cup buttermilk or low-fat yogurt

½ tablespoon minced onion

Dash freshly ground pepper

Paprika

Fresh, minced parsley

Scrub potatoes in cold water with vegetable brush. Pierce each potato in several places with fork. Bake at 400 degrees for 45 minutes or until tender.

Cut hot potatoes in half lengthwise. Scoop out inside of potato, leaving skins intact for restuffing. With wire whisk, beat potato with remaining ingredients, except paprika and parsley, until fluffy. Do not add too much liquid as mixture can become runny.

Put mixture back into skins; sprinkle with paprika and parsley. Bake 10 minutes or until golden brown.

Ralph E. Becker

Rosemary Potatoes

SERVES 6

2 pounds red potatoes, cut into ¼-inch slices

2 tablespoons olive oil

3 tablespoons fresh rosemary, chopped

Preheat oven to 450 degrees. Oil two large baking sheets. Arrange potatoes in one layer and brush with olive oil. Sprinkle rosemary, salt and pepper on top.

In upper third and lower third of the oven, roast the potatoes for 10 minutes. Switch position of the sheets and continue to roast another 10 minutes. The potatoes should be golden brown.

Cookbook Committee

Manon's Shoelaces

SERVES AS NEEDED

2 small potatoes per person

2 tablespoons olive oil

Williams Sonoma French Fry Salt

Salt and pepper to taste

Use an apple peeler/corer to make shoestring potatoes. Suggest scrubbing, not peeling the potatoes. Heat a large, non-stick pan, add 2 tablespoons olive oil, then the potatoes. Shake a generous amount of the Williams Sonoma salt on the potatoes, and cook over medium heat, stirring and turning often to brown evenly on all sides. If the potatoes appear dry, add another splash of oil. Season to taste. They cook quickly, in 10-15 minutes.

You can make this recipe with sweet potatoes as well, or with apples (cored and sliced) — but do not use French Fry Salt with apples!

Yvonne Caruthers
NSO Cello

Spinach Secret Surprise

SERVES 8

2 10-ounce packages frozen chopped spinach

1½ 14-ounce cans artichoke hearts, drained

¾ cup (1½ sticks) butter, divided

1 8-ounce package cream cheese

1 egg, beaten

1 8-ounce can sliced water chestnuts

Garlic salt to taste

Cayenne pepper to taste

1 cup bread crumbs

Cook spinach and drain. Melt 1 stick of butter. Add cream cheese, spinach, water chestnuts, beaten egg, garlic salt and cayenne pepper. Cut artichokes in half and line a greased baking dish with artichoke hearts. Reserve a few to decorate top if desired. Melt ½ stick butter and stir in bread crumbs. Fill baking dish with spinach mixture and cover with stuffing.

Bake uncovered at 400 degrees for 20 to 25 minutes. Can easily be increased or doubled by proportionately increasing ingredients.

Dorothy Pierce McSweeny
NSO Board Member

Stuffed Zucchini Pike Place Market

SERVES 6 TO 8

6 large zucchini

3 tablespoons olive oil

3 medium onions, minced

3 cloves garlic, mashed

10 parsley sprigs, leaves only

½ teaspoon salt

1 teaspoon black pepper, freshly ground

½ teaspoon garlic salt

½ cup fresh basil leaves (cut into strips) or 2 tablespoons dried basil

2 pounds Italian sausage (mix them up, hot and mild)

3 slices sourdough bread

¾ cup milk

¾ cup Parmesan cheese, grated

Italian salad dressing

Zucchini should be about 2½ inches thick and approximately 6 to 7 inches long. Cut off stems and parboil whole in boiling, salted water for about 12 minutes. Drain and cool.

Cut zucchini lengthwise into halves. Scoop out pulp and set aside.

Place olive oil in a skillet and heat. Add onions, garlic, parsley and basil. Sauté for about 4 minutes.

Remove sausage from its casing and place meat, broken into small pieces, in mixture. Add salt, pepper, garlic salt and other seasoning. Cook for about 15 minutes. Remove from heat.

Preheat oven to 350 degrees. Soak sourdough bread in milk until milk is absorbed; squeeze out milk from bread and shred bread. Add shredded bread, cheese and zucchini pulp to skillet with sausage mixture. Blend well for about 3 minutes.

Stuff zucchini with mixture. Oil baking pan with olive oil, arrange zucchini in pan and sprinkle with a few drops of olive oil over top. Bake for approximately 30 minutes.

Immediately before serving, spoon about 1 tablespoon salad dressing over each zucchini. Zucchini may be served hot or cold.

Llewelyn G. Pritchard

Turnips Bordelaise

Serves 6

2 pounds white turnips

4 tablespoons butter

Salt and freshly ground pepper

Water, about ½ cup

2 cloves garlic

1 shallot

½ cup coarse bread crumbs

1 tablespoon minced parsley

Peel turnips and cut into walnut-size pieces. Melt 3 tablespoons of butter. Add turnips, salt and pepper to taste, and a small amount of water. Cover pan and cook slowly over low heat until turnips are cooked through and liquid has been absorbed.

Mince garlic and shallot; mix with bread crumbs and parsley. Add 1 tablespoon butter to pan. Add bread crumb mixture and toss turnips to coat. Brown briefly over moderately high heat, shaking pan often.

Pamela Powers
Former NSO FANS Member

Christmas Tomatoes

Serves 6

6 medium large tomatoes

10-ounce package frozen spinach (chopped)

½ cup (1 stick) butter

1 bunch (6-8) spring onions

1-1½ cups bread crumbs

¾ cup grated Parmesan cheese

1½ teaspoons dried basil

1 teaspoon dried oregano

1 tablespoon fresh parsley, chopped

Cook spinach in small amount of water to thaw. Drain. Squeeze out moisture so spinach is dry. Cut off stem ends of tomatoes and scoop out pulp (leaving ½-inch shell). Sprinkle inside of tomatoes with salt and invert on rack. Reserve pulp.

In skillet, melt butter. Sauté chopped spring onions with basil, oregano and parsley. Add spinach and ½ cup tomato pulp (chopped) and heat through. Add bread crumbs so mixture holds together but is not dry. Add Parmesan cheese and mix well.

Stuff tomatoes with stuffing mix. Sprinkle top with Parmesan. Place in lightly-oiled Pyrex dish just large enough to hold tomatoes.

Bake for 20 to 25 minutes at 350 degrees.

Joan H. Lewis

Tomato Casserole

SERVES 8

This recipe was served on April 22, 1999 at a reception at the home of NSO National Trustee Doyce Hancock Deas honoring the National Symphony Orchestra's Residency in Mississippi.

2 16-ounce cans of diced tomatoes

½ cup chopped onion

¼ cup chopped bell pepper

¾ to 1 cup of light brown sugar

1 tablespoon Worcestershire sauce

¾ teaspoon Creole seasoning

1 cup Pepperidge Farm Cornbread stuffing

1 cup grated sharp cheddar cheese, optional

Combine diced tomatoes, chopped onion, chopped bell pepper, light brown sugar, Worcestershire sauce, Creole seasoning and Pepperidge Farm cornbread stuffing. Pour into a 9x13-inch baking dish. Bake at 350 degrees for 25 minutes or until hot and bubbly. Top with grated sharp cheddar cheese if desired.

Doyce Hancock Deas
NSO National Trustee

Stuffed Mushrooms

SERVES 6

12 very large fresh mushrooms

½ pound Italian ricotta cheese

2 eggs

½ cup cracker crumbs

½ cup raw wheat germ

Chopped fresh parsley to taste

1 teaspoon chopped basil to taste

1 heaping tablespoon Romano grated cheese

Salt and freshly ground pepper to taste

Chopped garlic or onion (optional)

Wash mushrooms, remove stems and chop, reserving them for later. Oil large pan and put in mushrooms, being sure cap side is down; sauté lightly.

Mix together ricotta, eggs, cracker crumbs, raw wheat germ, parsley, basil, grated cheese, salt and pepper. (Remember that the cheese is very salty.) Add reserved chopped mushrooms to filling.

Fill caps, mounding slightly. Grate more cheese on top, sprinkle with a dash of paprika and drizzle over tops a little olive oil.

Bake in oven 15 to 20 minutes at 400 degrees. Chopped garlic or onion is also good in filling. If filling is too dry, add more ricotta.

Mrs. Ramon Scavelli

Cucumbers Filled with Smoked Salmon Topped with a Citrus Tomato Jam

SERVES 12

CITRUS TOMATO JAM

12 ounces peeled tomatoes, canned

2 tablespoons garlic

2 tablespoons shallots

1 lemon (juice and zest)

1 orange (juice and zest)

1 cup white wine

Pinch of saffron, optional

1 cucumber

12 ounces smoked salmon

Olive oil

Salt and pepper to taste

Make the citrus jam first. Strain and seed the canned tomatoes and roughly chop. In a pot, quickly sauté the garlic and shallots and deglaze the pan with white wine. Add tomatoes, zest and juice and simmer until all the liquid has reduced. Then chill.

Peel the cucumber and cut into 2-inch rings. Make sure to hull out the center of the cucumber rings. Finely dice the smoked salmon; season with olive oil, salt and pepper. Fill the cucumber with the smoked salmon and top with the citrus tomato jam.

Chef Fabrizio Aielli
Teatro Goldoni Restaurant

Wild Mushroom Bread Pudding

SERVES 6 TO 8

3 tablespoons olive oil

6 ounces shitake mushrooms

6 ounces oyster mushrooms

6 ounces crimini mushrooms

2 large portobello mushrooms

4 teaspoons chopped garlic

1 tablespoon chopped fresh basil

1 tablespoon chopped fresh parsley

1 teaspoon dried sage

1 teaspoon dried thyme

5 large eggs

2 cups heavy cream

1 cup whole milk

¼ cup grated Parmesan cheese

¾ teaspoon salt

½ teaspoon pepper

6 cups stale challah

Preheat oven to 350 degrees. Saute mushrooms, garlic and herbs in oil. Cool and add salt and pepper to taste.

Whisk eggs, cream, milk, Parmesan cheese, salt and pepper. Toss in stale bread and let stand at least 15 minutes. Stir in mushroom mixture and sprinkle top with additional Parmesan cheese.

Bake at 350 degrees for 40 minutes or until center springs back to the touch.

Carole Ash
The Artful Party

Pissaladière Provençal (Onion and Tomato Tart)

SERVES 6 TO 8

1 partially baked 9 or 10-inch tart shell

4 tablespoons butter

3 pounds onions (to make 6 cups), finely chopped

2-3 peeled garlic cloves, finely chopped

2 tablespoons olive oil

2 pounds fresh tomatoes, peeled, seeded, juiced and chopped

1 tablespoon tomato paste

2 teaspoons dry basil

1 teaspoon oregano

1 teaspoon salt

Freshly ground pepper

1 tablespoon dry bread crumbs

24 flat anchovies, drained

24 black olives

1 tablespoon olive oil

1 tablespoon Italian parsley, finely chopped

Filling is also delicious over broiled fish or chicken.

Melt butter in 10 to 12-inch skillet over moderate heat. Stir in onions and when well coated with butter, simmer for 10 minutes covered. Stir occasionally.

Uncover after 10 minutes. Add garlic and cook for 30 minutes over low heat, stirring occasionally until all liquid is evaporated and onions are translucent.

Put olive oil in another pan and set over high heat. Add chopped tomatoes and bring to a boil. Stir frequently and let boil until almost all liquid is gone. Remove from heat; stir in oregano, basil and tomato paste. Combine onions and tomatoes; add salt and pepper. Taste for seasonings.

Preheat oven to 375 degrees. Place partially cooked pastry shell (still in its tart pan) on a cookie sheet. Spread bread crumbs in bottom to absorb any excess liquid and prevent a soggy shell. Spoon in onion and tomato mixture and smooth to edges of crust. Make a lattice work of anchovies across tart. Place an olive in each resulting square. Dribble one tablespoon olive oil on top.

Bake in center of oven for 30 minutes or until onion and tomato mixture is lightly browned. Serve either hot or at room temperature. Sprinkle with chopped parsley just before serving.

The onion mixture can be prepared earlier in the day, as can the pastry shell, and combined just before baking.

Mrs. Harry E. Gould

The National Symphony Orchestra performs at the Watergate Concert Shell on the Potomac River (1930s). Credit The Washington Post.

Note: *recipes marked with this icon are from the original National Symphony Orchestra Cookbook, published by FANS (Friends Assisting the National Symphony) in 1983.*

SAUCES & RELISHES

SAUCES & RELISHES

Fresh Tomato Sauce

MAKES 4 CUPS

1 clove garlic, minced

½ cup onions, finely chopped

3 tablespoons olive oil

¼ cup celery, finely chopped

3 cups diced, ripe tomatoes or 1 large can Italian-style tomatoes

½ teaspoon sugar

1 teaspoon salt

Freshly ground pepper to taste

1 teaspoon dried basil or 1 tablespoon fresh basil

1 small bay leaf

2 tablespoons tomato paste

Sauté garlic and onion in olive oil in heavy pan. Add celery, diced tomatoes, sugar, salt, pepper and bay leaf. Cook mixture for 20 minutes. Press through coarse sieve. Stir in tomato paste and heat.

Cookbook Committee

Bar-B-Sauce

MAKES ENOUGH FOR 2 POUNDS OF MEAT

3 tablespoons olive oil

3 tablespoons soy sauce

3 tablespoons ketchup

1 tablespoon vinegar

1 teaspoon ground black pepper

1 teaspoon sugar

3 cloves garlic, chopped small

Put all ingredients in a bowl and mix until oil is absorbed. Brush on lamb, chicken, flank steak or fish. If meat is barbequed, brush on as meat cooks.

Kathleen McGuth
NSO Women's Committee Member

Pesto-Genoese Fresh Basil Sauce

MAKES 1 CUP

2 cups fresh basil leaves

½ cup olive oil

2 tablespoons pine nuts (blanched almonds may be substituted)

2 cloves mashed garlic

1 teaspoon salt

⅔ cup freshly grated Parmesan or 4 parts Parmesan to 1 part sharp Romano cheese

4 tablespoons butter

Put basil, olive oil, pine nuts, garlic and salt in a blender or food processor and mix at high speed. Stop from time to time and scrape ingredients down toward bottom of blender cup with a rubber spatula. Add grated cheese and butter; blend briefly.

Before spooning pesto over pasta, dilute pesto with a tablespoon or so of hot water in which pasta was boiled. If adding to other sauces, various liquids can be used to blend it.

To make pesto for freezer, mix all ingredients in blender but do not add cheese or butter. Spoon mixture into a jar and seal tightly; freeze. Before using, thaw overnight in refrigerator. Mix grated cheese and butter; add to completely thawed mixture.

Pesto may be added to soups, vegetable dressings, salad dressings and dips. A little goes a long way. Pesto can also stand in refrigerator a month or longer.

Cookbook Committee

Kosher Dill Cucumbers or Tomatoes

MAKES A LOT!

10 pounds small whole cucumbers or small round green tomatoes

Cloves of garlic

Hot red pepper pods

Peppercorns

Fresh dill

3 quarts water

1 cup salt

4 cups vinegar

Wash and dry vegetables and pack in sterilized quart jars. For each jar add 1 peeled clove garlic, 1 hot red pepper pod, 4 to 6 peppercorns and 1 generous sprig of fresh dill. Combine water, salt and vinegar in saucepan, bring to boil and pour at once over pickles. Seal jars.

David Howard
NSO Cello

Texas Sweet Pickles

MAKES ABOUT 1 QUART

5 large sour pickles, cut into rounds

4 tablespoons pickling spice

4 cups sugar

4 tablespoons oil

Put pickles in bowl, sprinkle with spices. Cover with sugar and pour on oil.

Cover and let stand overnight. Turn and let stand until it exudes its own juice.

Patrick Hayes
Former NSO General Manager

Janet's Dressing

SERVES 6

4 garlic cloves

Peeled fresh ginger the size of 2 thumbs

1 tablespoon curry powder

2 teaspoons mustard

2 tablespoons maple syrup, preferably Vermont grade B

½ cup olive oil

¼ cup balsamic vinegar

In a food processor, chop the garlic and ginger. Add the rest of the ingredients and process again.

The curry powder and mustard are optional. I love the maple syrup sweetener but regular sugar or even sugar substitute will work fine too. This dressing works great as a marinade for stir fry also.

Janet Frank
NSO Cello

Cranberry Compote

SERVES 6 TO 8

2 packages Stouffer's frozen harvest apples

1 medium can whole cranberries

1 small package chopped walnuts

Let apples defrost at room temperature. Place in casserole. Add cranberries and nuts. Mix well. Bake at 350 degrees for about 35 minutes. Do not cover while baking in oven. Serve at room temperature.

Rhoda Silverman
NSO Women's Committee Member

The National Symphony Orchestra performs on the Ellipse at the White House. Photo from NSO Archives.

Note: *recipes marked with this icon are from the original National Symphony Orchestra Cookbook, published by FANS (Friends Assisting the National Symphony) in 1983.*

CAKES & TORTES

Michael Kaiser's Cherry Almond Cake

SERVES 8

½ cup butter

2½ cups sugar

2 eggs

1 cup flour

1¼ teaspoons baking powder

2 tablespoons almond extract

1 can red tart pitted cherries

Confectioners sugar

Preheat oven to 400 degrees. Butter an 8-inch or 9-inch springform pan. Cream butter and sugar together. Mix in eggs, flour, baking powder and almond extract. Spread evenly in pan.

Drain can of red tart pitted cherries well and place on top of batter. Bake at 400 degrees for one hour or until golden brown and a cake tester comes out clean. Let cool. Remove from spring pan. When completely cooled, sprinkle with confectioners sugar.

Michael M. Kaiser
President, The John F. Kennedy Center for the Performing Arts

Stephen Dumaine's Apple Cake

SERVES 8

2 cups sugar

1½ cups oil

3 eggs

3 cups flour

¾ teaspoon salt

1½ teaspoons baking soda

½ teaspoon cinnamon

½ teaspoon nutmeg

½ teaspoon cloves

3 cups diced apples with skin on

1 cup chopped nuts

Beat eggs and oil. Add sugar and continue beating. Add flour, salt, baking soda, cinnamon, nutmeg and cloves. Fold in apples and nuts.

Bake in greased tube or bundt pan sprinkled with sugar for 1½ hours at 350 degrees.

Stephen Dumaine
NSO Principal Tuba

Mildred's Apple Cake

SERVES 12 TO 15

4 cups plus 2-3 extra apples, cut in wedges

2 tablespoons sugar

1½ teaspoons cinnamon

1 cup raisins

3 cups flour

1 tablespoon baking powder

1 teaspoon salt

2 cups sugar

4 eggs

1 cup oil

¼ cup orange juice

2½ teaspoons vanilla

Goes anywhere, always looks nice, is very moist, and stays fresh a long time.

Preheat oven to 350 degrees. Mix 2 tablespoons sugar with cinnamon and sprinkle over apples. Add more sugar if necessary. Add raisins and set aside.

Sift flour with baking powder and salt. Cream sugar and eggs. Add oil, orange juice and vanilla to creamed mixture. Stir in dry ingredients.

Put half batter in greased tube pan. Add half apple mixture. Cover apples with remaining batter. Top batter with remaining apples. Be careful not to let apple mixture touch sides of pan; it might stick.

Bake at 350 degrees for 1½ hours or longer.

Carol Sue Lebbin
Former NSO FANS Member

Janet's Harvest Cake

SERVES 12 TO 15

4 cups diced and peeled apples

2 cups sugar

3 cups flour

2 eggs

1 cup cooking oil

1 teaspoon salt

1 teaspoon cinnamon

1 teaspoon nutmeg

2 teaspoons baking soda

1 teaspoon vanilla

1 cup chopped walnuts

Mix apples and sugar; let stand for 1 hour. Sift flour, baking soda and spices. Beat eggs, oil and vanilla together; add to apples. Stir in flour mixture and walnuts.

Bake in greased and well-floured tube or bundt pan at 350 degrees for 1 hour or until done.

Anne Merick
Variation: Use 1½ cups whole wheat flour, 1½ cups regular flour and ½ cup white sugar combined with ½ cup brown sugar.

John Berg
Former NSO Administrative Staff Member

Best Carrot Cake Ever

SERVES 12

2 cups sugar

1½ cups salad oil

4 eggs, well beaten

2 cups flour

2 teaspoons baking soda

2 teaspoons baking powder

2 teaspoons cinnamon

1 teaspoon salt

1 cup chopped pecans

3 cups grated, raw carrots (1 pound)

FROSTING
8-ounce package cream cheese

½ cup chopped pecans

¼ cup butter

1 box confectioners sugar

2 teaspoons vanilla

Mix together sugar and salad oil. Add well-beaten eggs and mix. Combine dry ingredients and add egg-oil mixture. Stir until smooth. Add chopped nuts and grated carrots. Bake in 3 greased, 9-inch, layer pans at 325 degrees for about 30 minutes. For 2 pans, bake a few minutes longer.

FROSTING
Combine cream cheese with butter and sugar. Add nuts and vanilla. Mix well. Frosts a 3 layer cake.

Sybil Amitay, Jane Stein & Anne Wesson
Former NSO FANS Members

Pumpkin Cake

SERVES 12 TO 20

Good as breakfast bread.

4 cups unbleached flour

1 teaspoon salt

2 rounded teaspoons baking powder

2 rounded teaspoons baking soda

4 teaspoons cinnamon

½ teaspoon powdered ginger

¼ teaspoon powdered cloves

¼ teaspoon nutmeg

¼ teaspoon allspice

1½ cups raisins

2 cups walnuts, chopped

2 cups plain, canned pumpkin

2¼ cups sugar

1¼ cups sunflower oil

7 large eggs, at room temperature

Preheat oven to 350 degrees. Grease 12-cup bundt pan. Sift together first 4 ingredients; stir in spices.

In large bowl of electric mixer place pumpkin, sugar and oil. Beat at medium speed until smooth. Add eggs, one at a time, beating after each addition. Beat mixture at medium speed until bubbles form.

Fold in flour-spice mixture. Fold in raisins and nuts. Pour into prepared pan and level off with spatula.

Bake for 1 hour or until done. Do not open oven door until cake has baked at least 45 minutes. Cool upright for 10 minutes; then invert onto rack.

Lewis Lipnick
NSO Contrabassoon

Cherry Almond Cake

SERVES 8

2 cups drained, canned sour cherries (not cherry pie filling)

1¼ cups sugar

½ cup chopped or sliced almonds

2 eggs, well beaten

1 cup flour

¾ cup melted unsalted butter

1 teaspoon almond extract

Preheat oven to 325 degrees. Place cherries on the bottom of a 10 or 11-inch pie plate. Sprinkle cherries with a mixture of the almonds and ½ cup of the sugar. Add the remaining sugar (¾ cup) to the eggs, beating well. Beat in the flour, melted butter and almond extract. Pour over the cherry mixture.

Bake for approximately one hour or until the crust is golden. Cool until room temperature on a rack. Serve plain, cut in wedges, or with vanilla ice cream.

Caryl Bernstein
NSO Board Member

Date Cake

Serves 10 to 12

♫

½ cup (1 stick) butter

1 cup sugar

1 egg

1 cup cake flour

1 teaspoon vanilla

1 cup chopped dates

1 cup boiling water

1 teaspoon baking soda

½ cup chopped pecans

1 teaspoon cinnamon

Cream butter, sugar and egg. Beat in flour, vanilla and cinnamon. Set aside.

In another bowl, mix dates, boiling water and soda. Let stand for 10 minutes. Add to creamed mixture. Stir in nuts.

Pour into well-greased, 8-inch square pan and bake at 375 degrees for 30 minutes.

Delicious and moist. Serve warm with dollop of whipped cream.

JoAnn Mason
Former NSO FANS Member

Strawberry Shortcake Torte

Serves 12

♫

9 egg whites

1½ cups sugar

¾ cup blanched almonds, finely chopped or ground

1 teaspoon vanilla

1 quart strawberries, cut and sugared

1 pint heavy cream, whipped

In large bowl, at room temperature, beat egg whites until stiff and dry. Add sugar gradually and continue beating. Add vanilla and fold in almonds. Spread evenly in 2 buttered and floured cake pans; bake at 325 degrees for 25 to 30 minutes.

When cool, split layers; put strawberries and whipped cream between layers and on top. Garnish cake with whole strawberries and whipped cream. Refrigerate. Best when made day of serving.

Mrs. Max Rudolf
Wife of Guest Conductor, Max Rudolf

Cap's Cake

SERVES 12 TO 15

Serve very thin slices to very thin people!

CAKE
¼ pound butter, softened

1 cup sugar

½ cup milk

1⅔ cups cake flour

2 teaspoons baking powder

2 egg whites

1 teaspoon vanilla

CHOCOLATE FILLING
2 squares bitter chocolate, melted

¼ pound butter

Pinch salt

2 tablespoons Kahlua or brandy

½ cup light cream

2 egg yolks

5 cups confectioners sugar

SEMI-SWEET CHOCOLATE ICING
3 squares bitter chocolate

1 teaspoon vanilla

¼ cup boiling water

2 tablespoons butter

1 cup confectioners sugar

Blanched almonds, for garnish

CAKE
Combine butter, sugar, milk, flour, baking powder, egg whites and vanilla in a large mixing bowl; beat at low speed, scraping often, until smooth and well blended. Increase speed to high and beat for 3 minutes. Pour into 2 greased, 9-inch, round pans and bake for about 20 to 25 minutes at 350 degrees. Cool slightly and turn out onto cake rack. When cakes are cooled, split each into 2 layers.

CHOCOLATE FILLING
In mixing bowl cream butter, salt and yolks. Add cream mixture to cooled chocolate. Beat well. Continue beating while adding sugar, a little at a time. Add brandy or Kahlua and beat at high speed until thoroughly creamed and light.

CHOCOLATE ICING
Melt chocolate and butter. Add water and vanilla and beat in confectioners sugar to make glossy, smooth icing.

TO ASSEMBLE
Place one split cake layer on plate, top with filling and repeat, ending with last cake layer. Frost top and sides with icing and decorate with blanched almonds.

Jane Weinberger

Helene Berman's Best Devil's Food Cake

SERVES 12 TO 14

CAKE

¼ pound butter

2 scant cups superfine sugar

2 eggs

1 scant teaspoon salt

1 teaspoon baking powder

3 full cups cake flour

2 cups buttermilk

2 scant teaspoons baking soda

2 squares semi-sweet baking chocolate

1 teaspoon vanilla

ICING

1 cup water

1 teaspoon butter

2 squares semi-sweet baking chocolate

½ cup superfine sugar

1 heaping tablespoon cornstarch

1 teaspoon vanilla

CAKE

Cream butter and gradually add sugar. Add eggs, one at a time. Sift flour 3 times; then add salt and baking powder. Melt chocolate. Sift baking soda into buttermilk and stir. Add melted chocolate to creamed mixture; then add vanilla. Add flour and buttermilk to creamed mixture alternately, beginning and ending with flour. Beat at low speed.

Grease a 13x9x2-inch pan and line with wax paper. Pour batter into pan and bake at 350 degrees for 45 to 50 minutes or until toothpick inserted in center comes out dry. Cool on rack for 15 minutes, turn out on tray and remove wax paper.

ICING

Melt butter and chocolate in water over low heat. Mix cornstarch into sugar. Add gradually to butter-chocolate mixture, stirring until it thickens like chocolate pudding and comes to a boil. Remove from heat and add vanilla. Stir until smooth. Frost cake when cool.

Helene Berman
Former NSO FANS Member

Chocolate Mousse Cake 1789

SERVES 8 TO 10

PASTRY CREAM
6 egg yolks

¾ cup granulated sugar

6 tablespoons flour

2⅓ cups milk

1 teaspoon vanilla

CHANTILLY CREAM
1 cup cold heavy cream

3 tablespoons confectioners sugar

CHOCOLATE COUVERTURE
5 ounces semi-sweet chocolate

RUM SYRUP
⅓ cup water

2 tablespoons granulated sugar

3 tablespoons rum

CHOCOLATE GENOISE
½ cup flour

½ cup sugar

½ cup cocoa powder

5 eggs

1 teaspoon vanilla

PASTRY CREAM
In a bowl, mix egg yolks with sugar and flour. Bring milk to a boil in a saucepan. Gradually stir boiling milk into egg yolk mixture. Pour hot milk mixture back into saucepan and place over low heat, stirring constantly until it thickens. Do not allow mixture to boil. Stir in vanilla. Pour thickened mixture into bowl and chill.

CHANTILLY CREAM
Whip cream with chilled beaters until doubled in volume. Add sugar and beat until soft peaks form. Refrigerate.

CHOCOLATE COUVERTURE
Place chocolate in top of double boiler and melt over low heat. Remove from heat. Set aside.

RUM SYRUP
In a small saucepan over high heat dissolve sugar in water. Bring to boil, remove from heat and stir in rum.

CHOCOLATE GENOISE
Butter a 9-inch cake pan (3-inch deep). Line bottom of pan with a wax paper round; butter paper and dust with flour. In a small bowl beat eggs and sugar at slow, medium, then high speed for 4 to 5 minutes. Reduce mixing speed and gradually beat in flour and cocoa. Pour into prepared pan and bake at 350 degrees for 25 minutes or until a toothpick inserted comes out clean. Cool in pan for 10 minutes, unmold and remove wax paper. Freeze 1 hour; then slice into 3 layers.

continued...

To Assemble

Fold together pastry cream, Chantilly cream and chocolate couverture in large bowl to make mousse filling. Refrigerate for at least 3 to 4 hours.

Place bottom layer of cake, cut side up, on cake plate and brush with rum syrup. Spread mousse in thick layer, add second layer and repeat process. Top with third layer and brush with remaining rum syrup. Ice top and sides of cake with remaining mousse. Chill a few hours.

Chef Pierre Dupont
1789 Restaurant

Chocaholic Bourbon Cake

SERVES 16 TO 18

This cake was made especially for the March 1983 NSO/WGMS Radiothon.

2 cups butter

1 cup granulated sugar

1 cup confectioners sugar

4 ounces unsweetened chocolate, melted

12 eggs, separated

1 teaspoon vanilla

1 cup chopped pecans

18 double ladyfingers

48 macaroons, broken and soaked in

½ to ⅔ cup bourbon

1 cup heavy cream, whipped

Cream butter, ½ cup granulated sugar and all confectioners sugar until light and fluffy. Beat egg yolks until light; blend into butter mixture. Beat in chocolate. Add vanilla and pecans.

Beat egg whites until fluffy; add remaining granulated sugar and beat until stiff but not dry. Fold into chocolate mixture.

Line sides and bottom of a 10-inch springform pan with split ladyfingers.

Soak macaroons in bourbon. Alternate layers of macaroons and chocolate mixture over ladyfingers in pan. Chill overnight.

Remove sides of pan and cover cake with whipped cream. This cake freezes well. Ice with whipped cream *after defrosting* however.

James D. Kraft
NSO Trombone

Grand Marnier Cake

SERVES 8 TO 12

CAKE

1 cup butter, at room temperature

1 cup sugar

3 eggs, separated

1 tablespoon Grand Marnier

2 cups sifted flour

¾ teaspoon baking powder

¾ teaspoon baking soda

1 cup sour cream

½ teaspoon grated orange rind

½ cup ground walnuts

SYRUP

¼ cup fresh orange juice

½ cup sugar

⅓ cup Grand Marnier

⅓ cup slivered, toasted almonds

Cream butter with sugar until light and fluffy. Add 3 egg yolks, one at a time, beating after each addition. Mix in Grand Marnier.

Sift flour, baking powder and baking soda. Add to butter mixture alternately with sour cream, using one third of dry ingredients and one half of sour cream each time. Stir in orange rind and nuts.

Beat egg whites until stiff but not dry. Fold mixture gently into egg whites.

Place in lightly buttered, 9-inch, tube pan and bake 50 to 55 minutes at 350 degrees.

SYRUP

Combine orange juice, sugar and Grand Marnier. Spoon over hot cake and let cake cool in pan before removing it. Stud top of cake with toasted, slivered almonds standing upright.

Gwen Holmes and Barbara Phillips
Former NSO FANS Members

Grandma Bryan's Bourbon Prune Cake

SERVES 12

2½ cups flour

1 teaspoon cinnamon

1 teaspoon nutmeg

1 teaspoon allspice

1 teaspoon baking soda

1 heaping teaspoon baking powder

¼ pound butter

2 cups sugar

4 eggs

1½ cups evaporated milk

1 pound pitted, cooked prunes, chopped

FROSTING

½ pound butter

1½ pounds confectioners sugar

Bourbon

Pecans

Preheat oven to 350 degrees. Sift together dry ingredients. Set aside. Cream butter and sugar. Add eggs one at a time. Mix in dry ingredients, alternating with evaporated milk and prunes. Grease and flour three 9-inch cake pans. Bake at 350 degrees for 30 to 35 minutes.

FROSTING

Cream butter and confectioners sugar. Add bourbon to spreading consistency. After frosting cake, sprinkle top with chopped pecans.

Tastes better if let set a day or two so the bourbon can ripen the cake.

Betty J. Bryan
NSO Women's Committee Member

East Texas Pound Cake

SERVES 12 TO 20

The pound cake that sold so well at the FANS Auction.

CAKE

½ pound (2 sticks) butter

1¾ cups sugar

5-6 eggs

2 cups sifted flour

1 teaspoon vanilla

RUM GLAZE

½ cup sugar

¼ cup water

1 ounce dark rum or
1 tablespoon rum extract

CAKE

Preheat oven to 325 degrees. Grease and flour tube pan or 2 standard loaf pans.

Cream together sugar and butter in bowl of an electric mixer. Add eggs, one at a time, beating well. Add flour slowly, again beating well. Add vanilla.

Bake at 325 degrees for about 1½ hours in middle of oven. Check after 1 hour. Cake is done when it leaves sides of pan. Cool in pan for 5 to 10 minutes; then turn out onto a rack. Cooking time should be shortened if using loaf pans; check after 45 minutes.

RUM GLAZE

Combine sugar and water in saucepan and bring to a bubbling boil. Boil for 3 seconds, remove from heat and add rum. Drizzle over cake while both are still warm.

Gus S. Morris
Former NSO FANS Member

Chocolate Chip Banana Bread

SERVES 8 TO 10

½ cup butter

1¼ cups sugar

2 eggs

¼ teaspoon salt

1½ teaspoons baking powder

½ teaspoon baking soda

4 tablespoons sour cream

2 medium size bananas, preferably over-ripe

2 cups flour

1 teaspoon vanilla

2 cups chopped walnuts

2 cups mini-size chocolate chips

2 small size loaf pans

Preheat the oven to 350 degrees. In a food processor chop the walnuts into small pieces. Set aside and wipe machine bowl clean.

Cream the butter and sugar in the food processor until well blended. Add eggs and salt. Mix well. Dissolve baking powder and baking soda in the sour cream and add to the above mixture. Add bananas and mix until thoroughly blended. Add the flour gradually, turning the food processor on and off.

Add walnuts and blend quickly. Add vanilla and blend. Pour in the chocolate chips, incorporating them in the batter.

Pour equal amounts into loaf pans. Do not grease. Bake 55 to 60 minutes. Cool on rack.

This banana bread freezes well.

—
Susan Porter
NSO Board Member

Sour Cream Pound Cake with Coconut

SERVES 10 TO 12

½ pound butter

3 cups sugar

6 eggs

3 cups cake flour

¼ teaspoon baking soda

2 teaspoons vanilla

1 cup sour cream

8 ounces grated coconut

Cream butter and sugar. Add eggs one at a time and beat after each addition. Sift flour and baking soda together. Add flour mixture alternately with sour cream. Add vanilla and coconut and mix well.

Bake in a large greased tube pan for 1½ hours at 350 degrees. Allow to cool in pan for 20 minutes.

Susan Popescu
NSO Women's Committee Member

Lemon Pudding Cake

SERVES 6

½ cup skim milk

½ cup buttermilk

3 egg yolks, lightly beaten

2 teaspoons canola oil

1 teaspoon lemon zest

⅓ cup fresh lemon juice

1 cup sugar

¼ cup flour

1 teaspoon cornstarch

⅛ teaspoon salt

3 egg whites

Preheat oven to 350 degrees. Blend the skim milk, buttermilk and the lightly beaten egg yolks. Add the canola oil, lemon zest, lemon juice and sugar. Mix in the flour and the cornstarch. Beat the egg whites and salt to soft peaks. Fold the whites carefully into lemon mixture.

Spray 6 4-ounce soufflé dishes with Pam. Dust with sugar. Fill with lemon mixture. Place soufflé dishes in baking dish half-filled with warm water (bain-marie).

Bake at 350 degrees for 30 minutes. Chill. Invert on plates to serve.

Cheris Garrison
NSO Women's Committee Member

Black Walnut Chiffon Cake

SERVES 16

1½ cups all-purpose flour

1 cup sugar

¼ teaspoon salt

2 teaspoons baking powder

6 eggs

¼ teaspoon cream of tartar

½ cup water

⅓ cup oil

1 teaspoon vanilla

¾ cup black walnut pieces (grind in food chopper to very fine consistency)

CARAMEL FROSTING

3 tablespoons butter

3 tablespoons milk

½ cup brown sugar, lightly packed

1½-2 cups confectioners sugar, sifted

½ teaspoon vanilla

Mix flour, sugar, salt and baking powder in a medium mixing bowl. Separate eggs into a small bowl of yolks and a large mixing bowl of whites. Add water, oil and vanilla to the egg yolks. Add the egg yolk mixture to the flour mixture and beat just until batter is smooth. Stir the finely ground black walnuts into the batter. Beat the egg whites with the cream of tartar until stiff peaks form. Gently fold the batter into the egg whites.

Place batter in an ungreased tube pan. Bake at 350 degrees for 15 minutes, then lower oven temperature to 325 degrees. Continue baking for 40 to 45 minutes. Cake is done when a light touch leaves no imprint and the cracks on the surface feel dry.

Remove from the oven and invert cake to cool. Use a long necked bottle to support the tube pans so the cake does not touch the surface.

CARAMEL FROSTING

In a saucepan combine butter, milk and lightly packed brown sugar. Heat and stir until the sugar is dissolved and mixture comes to a boil. Remove from the heat and stir in sifted confectioners sugar and vanilla. Beat until spreading consistency.

English walnuts or pecans can be substituted for black walnuts.

Marge Hoke
NSO Women's Committee Member

Cheesecake

CHEESECAKE
16 ounces cream cheese

4 large eggs

1 teaspoon vanilla

¾ cup sugar

CRUST
10 graham crackers

3 tablespoons melted butter

4 tablespoons sugar

½ teaspoon cinnamon

TOPPING
16 ounces sour cream

1 teaspoon vanilla

½ cup sugar

CRUST

Mix all of the ingredients in a food processor; then press 1½ cups of mixture into the bottom of a 9-inch springform pan. Reserve the balance of mixture.

CHEESECAKE

Mix cream cheese, eggs (one at a time) and add vanilla and sugar. Pour over crust. Bake at 300 degrees for 1 hour; then increase heat to 350 degrees.

TOPPING

Mix sour cream, vanilla and sugar and pour over top of cheesecake and bake 5 minutes at 350 degrees. Cake will be runny until cool. Cool to room temperature before refrigerating. Tastes best when prepared one day ahead and served chilled. Balance of crust mix may be used as garnish for the top of the cake when removed from the refrigerator.

Bill Brose

Pumpkin Cheesecake

SERVES 10 TO 12

CRUST

1½ cups graham cracker crumbs

3 tablespoons butter, melted

3 tablespoons sugar

FILLING

2 8-ounce packages cream cheese

1 cup heavy or light cream

1 cup pumpkin

¾ cup sugar

4 eggs, separated

3 tablespoons flour

1 teaspoon vanilla

1 teaspoon cinnamon

½ teaspoon ginger

½ teaspoon nutmeg

¼ teaspoon salt

TOPPING

1 cup sour cream

2 tablespoons sugar

½ teaspoon vanilla

For crust, combine ingredients and press into springform pan. Bake at 325 degrees for about 15 minutes.

For filling, combine all ingredients except egg whites and blend well. Beat egg whites and fold into cheesecake mixture. Pour into springform pan and bake at 325 degrees for 1 hour.

For topping, combine ingredients and pour evenly over baked cake. Return cake to 325 degree oven for 5 more minutes.

Debra Finlayson
Wife of Former NSO Assistant Principal Trombone

"Ton" Cake

SERVES 12 TO 16

½ pound butter

8 ounces cream cheese

2 cups sugar

2 teaspoons vanilla

2 teaspoons lemon juice or to taste

5 eggs, slightly beaten

2 cups self-rising flour

Cream together cream cheese and sugar. Mix with remaining ingredients for 3 minutes.

Bake at 350 degrees for 1 hour in a tube pan. This is a very rich and heavy cake.

Pamela Powers
Former NSO FANS Member

Cellist's Cheesecake

Serves 16

🎵

CRUST
16 Zwieback crackers, crumbled

¼ cup sugar

Dash of cinnamon

¼ cup butter, melted

FILLING
6 eggs

2¼ cups sugar

¼ cup flour plus 2 tablespoons

1 teaspoon salt

Juice of 1 lemon

1 teaspoon vanilla

3 pounds cream cheese

1½ cups light cream

This looming 6-inch high dessert, baked in an angelfood cakepan, was used at the NSO/WGMS Radiothon in March 1983.

Combine Zwieback crumbs, sugar, cinnamon and butter. Press into bottom of a 10-inch tube pan that has a removable bottom.

Beat eggs for 5 minutes, adding sugar gradually. Add flour, salt, lemon and vanilla.

In another bowl, beat softened cream cheese with cream until smooth, adding cream gradually after cheese is fluffy. Add egg mixture to cheese and keep beating.

Pour batter into crust and bake at 325 degrees for 1 hour. Open oven door after that and let cake stand in oven until cool (overnight is fine).

Refrigerate at least 8 hours before serving.

Yvonne Caruthers
NSO Cello

Praline Cheesecake

SERVES 10 TO 12

CRUST

1 cup graham cracker crumbs

3 tablespoons sugar

3 tablespoons butter, melted

FILLING

3 8-ounce packages cream cheese

1¼ cups packed dark brown sugar

2 tablespoons flour

3 eggs

1½ teaspoons vanilla

½ cup finely chopped pecans

8 pecan halves

¼ cup maple syrup

CRUST

Combine crumbs, sugar and butter; press onto bottom of 9-inch springform pan. Bake at 350 degrees for 10 minutes.

FILLING

Combine softened cream cheese, sugar and flour. Mix at medium speed until blended well. Add eggs one at a time, beating well after each addition. Blend in vanilla and chopped nuts. Pour mixture over crumbs.

Bake at 350 degrees for 50 to 55 minutes. Loosen springform ring but cool cake completely before removing it. Chill. Brush top with maple syrup and top with pecans halves.

Susan M. Carlson

Chocolate Ice Box Dessert

SERVES 8 TO 10

1 angel food cake	6 tablespoons water
6 eggs	2 teaspoons vanilla
12 ounces chocolate chips	1 teaspoon salt
4 tablespoons sugar	2 cups whipping cream

Line a flat 9x9-inch cake pan with wax paper. Slice angel food cake and place a layer of cake in pan. (Angel food cake slices better when frozen.)

Separate eggs; beat egg yolks.

Melt chocolate chips in a double boiler, add sugar and water, mix well, and be sure sugar melts.

Remove from heat and stir hot chocolate mixture gradually into beaten egg yolks and beat until smooth. Cool chocolate mixture completely. Add vanilla and salt and mix. Beat egg whites until stiff; whip cream. Fold egg whites into cooled chocolate mixture. Fold in whipped cream. Place a layer of chocolate mixture on sliced angel food cake, then another layer of cake, then a layer of chocolate.

Place in refrigerator and chill overnight. This may be frozen and used later. Be sure to chill overnight before freezing.

Mrs. Gerald Ford
Former First Lady

Coffee Honey Sponge Cake

SERVES 10 TO 12

1¾ cups honey

1 cup strong coffee

4 eggs

1 cup brown sugar

1 tablespoon vegetable oil

2 tablespoons water

3½ cups flour

1 tablespoon baking powder

1 teaspoon baking soda

1¼ teaspoons ground cinnamon

½ teaspoon ground cloves

½ teaspoon ground ginger

1 tablespoon grated lemon rind

Heat honey and coffee to boiling; cool completely. Sift dry ingredients together. Beat eggs well; add honey-coffee mixture, sugar, oil and water. Beat until completely blended.

Add flour mixture and beat until smooth. Pour batter into greased 10-inch tube pan. Bake at 300 degrees for 1 hour and 15 minutes or until top is golden. Cool in pan for 10 minutes; then turn out onto wire rack and cool completely.

Marcia Farabee
NSO Principal Librarian

COOKIES & CONFECTIONS

Apricot Hearts

MAKES ABOUT 2 DOZEN HEARTS

1 cup sifted flour

Pinch of salt

½ cup butter

4 ounces cream cheese

Apricot jam

1 egg

Into a bowl, sift flour and salt. Add butter and cheese. With pastry blender, cut butter and cheese into flour mixture until well blended. (Food processor does this beautifully.)

Lightly shape into ball, wrap dough in wax paper, and refrigerate until well chilled; otherwise, dough will get soft and sticky.

Heat oven to 400 degrees. Lightly grease 2 cookie sheets. On a floured board, roll out dough fairly thin. Cut into hearts.

Place 1 teaspoon of jam on half of hearts. Brush edges with beaten egg. Cover with another heart and press edges together.

Arrange on cookie sheets. Brush tops with beaten egg. Sprinkle with sugar and bake approximately 10 to 12 minutes.

Mrs. Eugene Ormandy
Wife of NSO Guest Conductor, Eugene Ormandy

Crunchy Lace Cookies

MAKES APPROXIMATELY 4 DOZEN

1 cup oatmeal

¾ cup sugar

3 tablespoons flour

½ teaspoon vanilla, lemon or almond extract

¼ teaspoon salt

½ teaspoon baking powder

½ cup (1 stick) butter

1 egg

Melt butter and pour over oatmeal, sugar, flour, extract flavoring, salt and baking powder. Add egg and mix well.

Drop by half teaspoons on foil about 3 to 4 inches apart (they will spread). Bake at 350 degrees for 7 to 9 minutes or until light brown. Leave on foil to cool.

Marilyn Erickson

Chocolate Nut Bars

MAKES 4 DOZEN

½ cup butter

1 cup brown sugar

1 cup white sugar

2 eggs

2 teaspoons vanilla

2 cups flour

½ teaspoon soda

½ teaspoon salt

1 cup semi-sweet chocolate chips

1 cup chopped nuts, optional

Cream butter and sugar. Add egg and vanilla. Beat well.

Sift together flour, salt and soda. Add to creamy mixture. Stir in chocolate chips and nuts.

Spread batter into 2 greased 11x7x2-inch pans. Push down; batter will rise. Bake 20 to 25 minutes at 375 degrees.

Cut into squares while warm.

Norma Dugger
Former NSO FANS Member

Date Sticks

SERVES 6 TO 8

1 cup sugar

4 tablespoons butter, softened

½ teaspoon salt

2 large eggs, beat whites and yolks separately

1 teaspoon baking powder

1 cup sifted flour

1 8-ounce package dates, cut into small pieces

1 cup chopped pecans

1 teaspoon vanilla

Confectioners sugar

Cream sugar, butter and salt. Add beaten egg yolks and mix together well. Add vanilla. Mix cut-up dates and pecans with flour and baking powder. Combine mixtures; fold in lightly beaten egg whites.

Bake at 325 degrees in buttered 8x8x2-inch square cake pan for 40 to 45 minutes or until done. Cut into 24 bars (sticks) while still warm. Roll in confectioners sugar. Place in air-tight container. These will keep in refrigerator for several weeks or in freezer for several months.

Jane Gough
NSO Women's Committee Member

Dorothy Stahl's Whiskey Balls

SERVES 24 TO 36

2 pounds vanilla wafers

1½ cups crushed pecans

1 cup confectioners sugar

½ cup white Karo syrup

¾ cup bourbon, whiskey or rum

Sifted confectioners sugar for rolling

Crush the wafers until fine. Mix with confectioners sugar and Karo syrup. Add liquor and pecans. Roll into balls. Roll again in sifted confectioners sugar.

Dotian Levalier
NSO Principal Harp

Dorothy Stahl
Former NSO Cello

Chocolate Shortbread Rounds

MAKES 9 DOZEN

1 cup butter, softened

2 cups packed brown sugar

2 large eggs

2 tablespoons vanilla extract

1 tablespoon baking powder

3½ cups all-purpose flour

2 cups grated bittersweet chocolate

In a large bowl cream together butter and brown sugar. Mix in eggs, vanilla and baking powder. Add 2 cups flour and the grated chocolate. Add remaining flour. Divide dough into four portions, shaping each into a log about 1½ inches in diameter. Wrap and refrigerate until firm.

To bake, preheat oven to 375 degrees (350 degrees for convection oven). Cut chilled dough into ¼-inch slices. Place one inch apart on lightly greased baking sheets. Bake 8 minutes or until edges are lightly browned. Remove from baking sheets; cool on racks.

Roberta A. Meredith
NSO Women's Committee Member

Vanillekipferl (Vanilla Crescents)

MAKES 60 PIECES

These cookies are a traditional Christmas fare that have become so popular that they are served all year round. The key ingredient is the vanilla sugar, which is not easily found in America, so I import it especially from Austria.

1 cup less 2 tablespoons of cold butter

2½ cups all-purpose flour, sifted

½ cup powdered sugar

½ cup blanched almonds, ground

2 egg yolks

½ teaspoon vanilla

Austrian vanilla sugar (a good substitute is Oetker Vanilla Sugar available at Dean & Deluca)

Cut the butter into the flour and sugar. Add the almonds, egg yolks and vanilla and work into a smooth dough. Chill for at least an hour. Roll the dough into finger-width strips and cut into 2-inch pieces. Roll each piece out until it is 3 inches long and curve it into the shape of a crescent.

Bake the crescents on a buttered baking sheet for about 20 minutes or until they are dry and faintly colored. Sprinkle a plate heavily with vanilla sugar. Carefully transfer the crescents with a spatula onto the plate. Sprinkle them again with the vanilla sugar.

Monika Tuerk

Black Walnut Cookies

MAKES 90 COOKIES

½ cup butter, softened

½ cup Crisco

2 cups light brown sugar, firmly packed

2 large eggs, lightly beaten

1 teaspoon vanilla

3 cups flour, unsifted

½ teaspoon salt

1 teaspoon baking soda

1 cup black walnuts, finely chopped

Using electric mixer, cream together butter, Crisco and brown sugar. Add eggs, one at a time, and vanilla. Mix until well combined. Measure flour, salt and baking soda and place in separate bowl. Add flour mixture gradually to butter, Crisco, brown sugar, eggs and vanilla. Stir in black walnuts.

Divide dough into three parts and refrigerate for at least an hour. Take out and shape dough firmly with hands into three long, smooth rolls, approximately 1½ inches in diameter. Wrap dough in long sheets of wax paper or plastic wrap, folding over ends to seal. Place in refrigerator overnight. Rolls can be reformed after dough has become hard.

Heat oven to 325 or 350 degrees. Cut rolls into ¼ or less inch slices and place on ungreased cookie sheet. Bake 10 minutes or until a very light brown. Do not overbake or cookies will become hard. Let stand on cookie sheet for several minutes before placing on racks or wax paper to cool. Store in air-tight container. These cookies will keep in freezer for several months.

Jane Gough
NSO Women's Committee Member

Auntie I's Mandelbrot

MAKES ABOUT 3 DOZEN

1½ cups flour

2 teaspoons baking powder

2 teaspoons almond extract

4 beaten eggs

1 cup sugar

¾ cup corn oil

1 cup coarsely chopped walnuts or pecans

Preheat oven to 350 degrees. Grease and flour 3 metal ice cube trays.

Mix all ingredients together. Divide batter into 3 parts and fill trays.

Bake until browned, about 20 to 30 minutes. Turn out tins on cutting board to cool. Cut the individual squares of pastry with a sharp knife.

Place slices on cookie sheet and return to a 350 degree oven to crisp and brown on both sides. Freezes and stores well.

Mrs. Joseph Weinstein

Meringue Mushrooms

SERVES 16

3 egg whites, at room temperature

¾ cup superfine sugar

2 ounces (2 squares) semi-sweet chocolate, melted

Optional ½ teaspoon Crisco added to melted chocolate

Pastry bag and ⅝ tube

Parchment paper

Cocoa for dusting

Preheat oven to 200 degrees. Beat egg whites to a firm peak so that they hold their shape.

Measure out 3 teaspoons of sugar (from ¾ cup) and sprinkle on the stiff egg whites. Beat again until thick. By hand, fold in the remaining sugar carefully and quickly.

Fill the pastry bag with the meringue mixture. With a little of the mixture, "glue" down the sides of the parchment paper to the baking sheet. Pipe stems and caps onto the sheet. Sprinkle with the superfine sugar and let stand a few minutes.

Bake a minimum of one hour or until firm. Remove from the paper. Assemble mushrooms with the melted chocolate using a palette knife to smooth out the base. Dust with cocoa to resemble "dirt."

Susan Porter
NSO Board Member

Armenian Butter Cookies

MAKES 4 TO 5 DOZEN

2 cups sifted flour

8 tablespoons sugar

½ pound butter

1 teaspoon vanilla

Cinnamon-sugar mixture

Mix first four ingredients together.

Divide pastry into 2 or 3 rolls. Wrap each roll in wax paper and refrigerate.

Slice into ¼-inch slices and place them onto cookie sheet. Sprinkle with a mixture of cinnamon and sugar. Bake at 350 degrees for about 10 minutes or until lightly brown.

JoAnn Mason
Former NSO FANS Member

Val's Brownies

MAKES 36 SMALL SQUARES

½ pound butter

4 ounces unsweetened chocolate

3 eggs

2 cups sugar

1-2 teaspoons vanilla (almond or mint can be substituted for second teaspoon vanilla)

1 cup flour

Melt butter and chocolate (do not boil). Beat eggs with sugar; add flavoring and melted butter-chocolate mixture. Gradually add flour. Do not over beat.

Preheat oven to 350 degrees. Pour batter into a greased 9x9-inch pan. Place in oven and bake at 350 degrees for 45 minutes.

Cool, cut into squares.

Valerie Lapcinski
Former NSO Administrative Staff Member

Orange Cookies

MAKES 4 TO 5 DOZEN

2 cups white sugar

1 cup butter

2 eggs

4 cups flour

1 teaspoon baking powder

1 cup sour cream

Juice and grated rind of 2 oranges and 1 lemon

1 teaspoon baking soda

Confectioners sugar

¼ cup (½ stick) butter

Orange and lemon juices, enough for preferred consistency

Cream together sugar and butter; add eggs. Sift dry ingredients, adding alternately with sour cream and juice mixture. Add flour last.

Drop by teaspoons onto a greased cookie sheet. Bake at 375 degrees for 12 to 15 minutes.

After removing from oven, let cool. Frost with topping of confectioners sugar, butter and juice mixed until preferred consistency.

Sally Hedrick
Former NSO FANS Member

Jimmy Carter's Peanut Brittle

MAKES 3½ POUNDS

3 cups granulated sugar

1½ cups water

1 cup white corn syrup

3 cups raw peanuts

2 tablespoons baking soda

¼ cup (½ stick) butter

1 teaspoon vanilla

Boil sugar, water and syrup until it spins thread; add peanuts. After adding peanuts, stir continually until syrup turns golden brown.

Remove from heat and add remaining ingredients. Stir until butter melts.

Pour quickly onto 2 cookie sheets with sides. As mixture begins to harden around the edges, pull until thin.

The Jimmy Carter Family
Former President of the United States

Chocolate Peanut Butter Cups

MAKES ABOUT 4 DOZEN SMALL CANDIES

⅓ cup creamy or super chunky peanut butter

⅓ cup butter, softened

1⅔ cups sifted confectioners sugar

12-ounce package semi-sweet or milk chocolate pieces, melted

Place miniature muffin cups on tray.

In medium bowl stir together peanut butter and butter until blended. Gradually stir in confectioners sugar.

Turn onto board. Knead until smooth. Press with hands or roll out to ½-inch thickness. Cut into ½-inch circles with small cookie cutter.

Spoon some chocolate into paper cups to cover bottom generously. Place one peanut butter circle on top of chocolate in each cup. Gently push down to coat sides. Spread additional chocolate over top, making sure sides are completely coated.

Chill until firm. Store in refrigerator.

Gene A. Burns

Hillary Rodham Clinton's Original Chocolate Chip Cookies

MAKES 7 DOZEN

1½ cups flour

1 teaspoon salt

1 teaspoon baking soda

1 cup shortening

1 cup brown sugar, packed

½ cup granulated sugar

1 teaspoon vanilla

2 eggs

2 cups old-fashioned rolled oats

2 cups (12-ounce package) semi-sweet chocolate chips

Preheat oven to 350 degrees. Grease baking sheets. Combine flour, salt and baking soda. In a separate bowl, beat together shortening, sugars and vanilla until creamy. Add eggs, beating until light and fluffy. Gradually beat in flour mixture and rolled oats. Stir in chocolate chips.

Drop batter by well-rounded teaspoon onto greased baking sheets. Bake 8 to 10 minutes at 350 degrees or until golden. Cool cookies on sheets on wire rack for 2 minutes. Remove cookies to wire rack to cool.

Hillary Rodham Clinton
Senator
Former First Lady

Chocolate Chip Cookies

MAKES 5 DOZEN

2¼ cups and 1 teaspoon all-purpose flour

1 teaspoon baking soda

½ teaspoon salt

1 cup (2 sticks) butter, softened

¾ cup granulated sugar

1 teaspoon vanilla extract

2 eggs

2 cups (12-ounce package) semi-sweet chocolate morsels

Preheat oven to 375 degrees. Combine flour, baking soda and salt in small bowl. Mix together butter and sugar. Beat in eggs (one at a time) and vanilla. Gradually beat in flour mixture. Stir in morsels.

Drop by rounded teaspoon onto ungreased baking sheets. Bake 9 to 11 minutes at 375 degrees. Do not over bake. Let stand for 2 minutes. Remove to wire racks to cool.

Marvin Hamlisch
NSO Principal Pops Conductor

Mint Squares

MAKES MANY SQUARES DEPENDING UPON HOW LARGE YOU SLICE THEM

1 cup sugar

1 cup butter

4 eggs

1 cup flour

½ teaspoon salt

1 teaspoon vanilla

16-ounce can chocolate syrup

2 cups confectioners sugar

½ cup butter

4 tablespoons crème de menthe

6-ounce package chocolate chips

6 tablespoons butter

"A little goes a long way."

Cream together sugar and butter. Add eggs, flour, salt, vanilla and chocolate syrup.

Bake in 9x13-inch greased pan for 30 to 40 minutes at 350 degrees. Cool.

Mix together confectioners sugar, butter and crème de menthe. Spread over cooled cake and refrigerate until top layer stiffens.

Melt chocolate chips and butter. Cool slightly and dribble on as frosting. Store in refrigerator, as they tend to melt if kept out of refrigerator for very long.

Remove from refrigerator; cut and serve.

Julie Smith

Espresso Brownies

SERVES 16

4 unsweetened baking chocolate squares

¾ cup unsalted butter (1½ sticks)

1 cup semi-sweet Nestle chocolate chunks

¼ cup liquid espresso coffee

½ cup all-purpose unbleached flour

½ teaspoon salt

¼ teaspoon baking powder

3 large eggs

1 cup granulated sugar

1½ teaspoons vanilla

1 cup semi-sweet chocolate chunks

1 teaspoon confectioners sugar

Set oven temperature at 350 degrees. In a double broiler, combine and melt chocolate squares, chunks (1 cup) and butter. Stir in espresso coffee. Cool to about 100 degrees.

In a separate small bowl, mix together flour, salt and baking powder and set aside. In a large bowl, combine eggs, sugar and vanilla. Beat for two minutes. Add into large bowl the chocolate sauce and stir well. Then mix the flour into the large bowl and stir well.

Pour into greased 9x13-inch baking dish. Bake in oven for 15 minutes. Take out and quickly sprinkle remaining chocolate chunks evenly over brownies. Return to oven for 10 to 12 minutes. Remove from oven when test toothpick comes out clean. Cool on rack. Sprinkle confectioners sugar through sieve on top of brownies.

James Deighan
NSO Viola

Forgotten Cookies

MAKES 18

2 egg whites

⅔ cup sugar

6 ounce package of chocolate chips

1 cup chopped pecans

Preheat oven to 350 degrees. Beat 2 egg whites until stiff. Slowly add sugar until peaks form. Fold in chocolate chips and chopped pecans. Drop teaspoon full onto ungreased cookie sheet. Put in oven and turn off oven and leave in overnight.

Katie Tardio
NSO Women's Committee Member

Kahlua Espresso Coffee Truffles

MAKES 5 DOZEN

Decaffeinated coffee may be substituted, but why bother?

12 ounces semi-sweet chocolate

1 egg plus 2 more egg yolks, all lightly beaten

8 ounces butter (salted or unsalted)

2 cups cocoa powder (finely sifted) plus more for "dusting"

2 cups confectioners sugar (finely sifted) plus more for "dusting"

1⅓ cups walnuts (or pistachios) finely chopped (maybe using a food processor)

¼ cup Kahlua or any other liquor of choice or strong espresso coffee (may use 2 tablespoons of Kahlua plus 2 tablespoons of espresso to equal ¼ cup total)

Several ounces grated chocolate

Break the semi-sweet chocolate into pieces and set them into a ceramic, glass or heat-proof bowl, which is placed on top of a pot of hot (not boiling) water. Melt the chocolate, stirring with a wooden spoon. When the chocolate is melted and smooth, take the bowl off the pot of hot water.

In a separate bowl or glass beaker, lightly beat one complete egg plus two more egg yolks. Melt the 8 ounces of butter in a saucepan. Then stir in the slightly beaten eggs, the 2 cups of cocoa powder, the 2 cups of confectioners sugar, only ⅔ cup of the chopped walnuts or pistachios and the ¼ cup of Kahlua or other liquor or espresso coffee.

Fold the mixture into the melted chocolate and then vigorously whisk the paste until smooth and creamy. Since the bowl with the chocolate is warm, you can set this bowl into another bowl filled with ice to help cool the combination of ingredients. Place the ceramic or glass bowl into the refrigerator and chill the paste until it is firm enough to shape by hand into truffle-sized balls. Allow one hour to cool sufficiently.

In a small baking pan, spread out more cocoa powder. In three separate bowls, spread out more confectioners sugar, more finely chopped walnuts or pistachios (maybe another ⅔ cup) and the grated chocolate.

Remove the thickened paste from the refrigerator. Be sure that the mixture is cool. Using a small spoon, scoop up some of the paste, forming each scoop into a "walnut-sized" ball in your hand. Dip all of these into the cocoa powder in the baking pan, rolling them in the cocoa powder to coat them completely.

continued...

Using the ingredients in the three soup bowls, coat ⅓ of these truffles with confectioners sugar, ⅓ with the finely chopped walnuts or pistachios and ⅓ with the grated chocolate.

Put each truffle into a separate Bon Bon size baking or party cup, or place them directly onto a serving plate, if preferred.

Decorate the serving plate with nuts, candied fruit, raisins, cherries, etc. Do not allow the truffles to stay in a warm environment. They should be kept cool until served.

Milt and Priscilla Stevens
NSO Principal Trombone

Syllabub

SERVES 6 TO 8

8-10 macaroons, bruttini or amaretti

1 cup confectioners sugar

1 cup heavy cream

¼ to ½ cup dark rum, sherry, bourbon, sweet wine or other spirits

¼ cup lemon juice

Powdered instant espresso coffee for dusting

Whirl macaroons or amaretti in food processor until finely crumbled. Set aside one cup of crumbs. Mix in confectioners sugar in food processor for a few seconds, add cream and process for about 1 minute. Blend in rum or other spirits and lemon juice. Turn into a bowl and refrigerate 1 to 2 days or freeze and defrost before serving.

When ready to serve fold in macaroon crumbs. Serve in chilled demitasse cups, syllabubs, glass syllabubs or other small glasses or cups. Dust with instant espresso coffee.

Marcia Feinstein

PASTRIES, PIES & FRUIT

Baklava à la Grecque

MAKES ABOUT 25 LARGE PIECES OR 50 SMALL ONES

SYRUP
5 cups sugar

3½ cups water

Lemon peel

1½ packages (about 26 ounces) phyllo

2 cups grated walnuts (do not crush or pulp nuts)

5 ounces white bread crumbs

1½ cups sweet butter, melted

Cinnamon

Cloves

Make syrup by mixing water, sugar, and lemon peel in a saucepan. Boil, stirring with a wooden spoon, for about 10 minutes. Remove from heat and allow to cool. Then add syrup to walnuts and bread crumbs, with cinnamon to taste. Blend well.

Brush bottom and sides of a baking pan measuring about 22x15x2 inches with melted butter. Place 6 sheets of phyllo on bottom of pan, brushing each sheet with melted butter. Care should be taken to keep unused phyllo sheets covered with a slightly damp towel while preparing pastry. Spread top sheet with syrup and nut mixture; then continue adding sheets of pastry until only 7 sheets are left, buttering each sheet and spreading each thinly, but evenly with mixture. Make sure mixture reaches all corners evenly. Put some melted butter around corners. Finish off with last 7 buttered sheets placed on top of each other without any syrup mixture.

Cut into pieces of desired size; place a single clove on each piece and bake at 280 degrees for 3 hours. Remove from oven and pour over remaining syrup which should be cold or lukewarm.

The pastry should not be eaten for at least 12 hours. It keeps well, without refrigeration, for about 3 weeks.

For cocktail parties, serve baklava in bite-size pieces placed in paper cups. Each piece should have its own clove.

Embassy of Greece

Pashka (Traditional Easter Dessert of Old Russia)

SERVES 16 TO 18

4 8-ounce packages cream cheese

1 cup butter

3 egg yolks

2 cups confectioners sugar

2 teaspoons vanilla

¾ cup candied citron, chopped

¾ cup slivered almonds, toasted

Strawberries

Let cream cheese, butter, and egg yolks stand at room temperature at least 2 hours before making pashka. Place cream cheese in a mixing bowl and beat with a wooden spoon. If an electric mixer is used, blend on low speed. Add butter and continue beating or blending on low speed. When well blended, add sugar, then egg yolks, one at a time. Add vanilla. Fold in citron and almonds.

Wash well and dry inside of a 2-quart clay or plastic flowerpot. There should be a hole in the bottom of the pot for drainage. Line pot with a double thickness of cheesecloth, wrung out in cold water. Spoon cheese mixture into pot, filling it to the brim. Cover with clear plastic wrap and refrigerate several hours or overnight.

To unmold, trim around and discard top of cheesecloth. Place a dessert plate over flowerpot and invert quickly. Gently lift off pot, tugging at a bit of cheesecloth lining, if necessary. When pot is clear, gently remove cheesecloth.

Garnish base of pashka with whole strawberries and strawberry halves. Serve with additional crushed, sweetened strawberries made into a sauce.

Dorothy Stahl
Former NSO Cello

Pineapple Millefeuille

SERVES 8 TO 10

Serve with Rum and Cider Grog.

FOR THE PINEAPPLE MOUSSE
4 gelatin sheets

1½ pineapples

1 cup of sugar and 1½ cups of water (to make light syrup)

FOR THE FRUIT PASTRY
½ pound of puff pastry

2 mangos

4 passion fruits

½ pineapple

2 bananas

2–4 tablespoons butter

1-2 tablespoons honey

Grated, toasted coconut

FOR THE RUM AND CIDER GROG
8 cups of cider

2 cups of water

1 cup of brown sugar

½ cup of honey (rhododendron)

1 stick of cinnamon

2 split vanilla beans

2 cloves

1 nutmeg pod

Fresh ginger to taste

Zest of 2 limes, save juice for later

Rum to taste

TO PREPARE THE PINEAPPLE MOUSSE
Soften 4 sheets of gelatin in cold water. Cut the pineapple in 10 sections and remove the core. Simmer the pineapple sections in light syrup for 20 minutes, mix in the blender and add the softened gelatin. Chill.

TO ASSEMBLE THE FRUIT PASTRY
Roll the puff pastry into a thin 2 to 3 mm (⅛ inch) rectangle measuring 10x15 inches. Bake at 380 degrees for 15 minutes or until golden brown. Peel and cut remaining fruit and sauté lightly in butter and 2 to 4 tablespoons of honey.

TO SERVE
Divide the millefeuille rectangle into four equal stacks and transfer the stacks to a dessert plate. Use a pastry bag or spoon to spread the pineapple mousse between each layer of millefeuille. Pile a mound of warm fruit on the side of each plate and garnish with toasted coconut. Place a slice of millefeuille on each plate.

TO PREPARE THE RUM AND CIDER GROG
In a large pot mix all ingredients except for lime juice and rum. Bring to a boil and remove from heat. Allow to steep 2 hours before straining.

Heat the grog just before serving and add the juice of 2 limes and rum. Serve in mugs.

Francis Layrle
Embassy of France

Grapefruit Tart with Chocolate Pecan Crust

SERVES 8

CRUST

2½ cups ground pecans (about 12 ounces whole pecans)

⅓ cup sugar

¼ cup or ½ stick unsalted butter, melted

2 ounces semi-sweet chocolate, melted

GRAPEFRUIT CUSTARD FILLING

¼ cup or ½ stick unsalted butter

¾ cup sugar

½ cup heavy cream

⅔ cup fresh grapefruit juice

½ cup fresh orange juice

4 eggs, lightly beaten

Grated zest of 1 grapefruit

2 teaspoons unflavored gelatin

GARNISHES

Whipped cream

Grapefruit sections

TO MAKE THE CRUST

In a small bowl, combine the pecans, sugar, and melted butter. Pat into a 9-inch Pyrex pie dish. Chill for 30 minutes in the refrigerator. Preheat the oven to 375 degrees. Bake the pecan crust for 10 minutes. Set aside to cool to room temperature. Using a pastry brush, spread the melted chocolate over the inside of the crust and set aside.

TO MAKE THE FILLING

In a 2-quart saucepan, melt the butter over medium heat. Add the sugar and stir until dissolved. Add the cream, ½ cup of the grapefruit juice, the orange juice, eggs and grapefruit zest. Sprinkle the gelatin over the remaining grapefruit juice to soften and set aside. Cook the cream-citrus mixture over low heat, stirring constantly, until it thickens and lightly coats the back of a spoon. Do not allow it to come to a boil, or the eggs may curdle. Add the gelatin mixture and stir until the gelatin is dissolved. When the custard is a cool room temperature, pour it into the chocolate-coated crust and refrigerate until set, about 2 hours.

TO SERVE

Cut the tart into wedges and garnish with the whipped cream and grapefruit sections.

This custard tart is at once startling and refreshing. The chocolate may be eliminated if you wish, and any other nut may be substituted for the pecans in the crust.

Chef Patrick O'Connell
The Inn at Little Washington

Palacsinta (Apricot Pancakes)

SERVES 6

3 eggs

1 cup milk

⅓ cup club soda, freshly opened

1 cup sifted flour

3 tablespoons granulated sugar

¼ teaspoon salt

1 teaspoon vanilla

4 tablespoons butter

¾ cup apricot jam

1 cup ground walnuts or filberts

Confectioners sugar

Beat eggs lightly with milk in a large mixing bowl. Combine with club soda. With a wooden spoon, stir in flour and sugar; then add salt and vanilla. Continue to stir until batter is smooth.

Melt 1 teaspoon butter in an 8-inch skillet until hot. Ladle in enough batter to cover bottom of skillet thickly and tilt skillet from side to side to spread batter evenly. Cook until lightly browned on one side; then turn and brown lightly on the other.

Spread 2 teaspoons of jam over pancake and roll it up loosely. Put it in a baking dish in a 200 degree oven to keep warm until all pancakes are rolled up. Serve warm as a dessert, sprinkle with nuts and confectioners sugar.

Bèla Màrtay
Former NSO Violin

Apple Crisp

SERVES 8

3 pounds thinly sliced tart apples

2 tablespoons lemon juice

¼ cup water

¾ cup flour

¾ cup rolled oats (not quick oats)

1½ cups brown sugar

¾ teaspoon ground nutmeg

¾ teaspoon ground cinnamon

¾ cup butter

1 cup coarsely chopped walnuts, optional

Toss apples with lemon juice and water in 13x9-inch glass baking dish. In a large bowl, combine flour, oats, sugar, nutmeg and cinnamon. Mix together. Cut in butter to resemble coarse crumbs. Add nuts and stir. Crumble oat mixture over apples to cover completely.

Bake 40 to 45 minutes at 350 degrees, until top is golden brown and apples are bubbling.

Serve warm with ice cream or whipped cream.

Christina Rossetti

Crepia aux Pommes

SERVES 6

8 apples

6 whole eggs

1 cup milk

¼ cup sugar

2 tablespoons flour

6 tablespoons butter

Applejack liqueur

Peel, core and slice apples very thin. Sauté rapidly in butter.

In a bowl, mix together flour, sugar and milk. Add eggs and blend to an even consistency.

Pour a thin layer of flour mixture into a hot, buttered crêpe pan. Next lay apples over flour mixture in pan as if on a tarte. Cover apples with another thin layer of mixture.

Place pan in a preheated 450 degree oven for 5 minutes. Remove from oven and slice onto plate. Flambé with applejack.

Chef Garard Vettraino
Jean-Pierre Restaurant

Blueberry Küchen

SERVES 8

1 cup flour

Pinch salt

2 tablespoons sugar

½ cup butter, softened

1 tablespoon vinegar

FILLING

3 to 4 cups blueberries (reserving 1 cup for garnish)

¼ cup sugar

1½ tablespoons flour

Several dashes of cinnamon

Preheat the oven to 400 degrees. Combine the pastry ingredients, except the vinegar, using a pastry cutter or two knives. Add vinegar. Spread in the bottom and 1 inch up the sides of a spring-form pan (other will do). Mix the filling ingredients together and pour onto the crust. Bake for 60 minutes.

Top with remaining cup of blueberries and confectioners sugar and serve with whipped cream or ice cream.

Holly Sukenik
Former NSO FANS Member

Bess Truman's Frozen Lemon Pie

SERVES 6 TO 8

3 eggs, separated

½ cup sugar

1 cup whipping cream

2 to 3 tablespoons grated lemon rind

⅓ cup lemon juice

Yellow coloring

1 cup graham cracker crumbs or cookie crumbs

Butter a 9-inch pan and sprinkle with cracker crumbs. Press down. Beat egg whites until frothy and gradually add sugar and a few drops of coloring. Continue to beat until stiff and glossy.

Beat egg yolks until thick and lemon colored, then fold carefully into egg whites. Beat cream until stiff and add lemon rind and juice. Mix well into egg mixture.

Pour into pie pan and sprinkle with ¼ cup fine cracker crumbs. Freeze.

Bess Truman
Former First Lady

Strawberry-Rhubarb Pie

SERVES 6 TO 8

Pastry for 9-inch double crust pie

3 cups sliced rhubarb

1 cup fresh, sliced strawberries

1 cup sugar

3 tablespoons flour

Line a 9-inch pie pan with pastry. Combine rhubarb, strawberries, sugar and flour. Pour into pie pan. Cover with top crust, making several slits for steam to escape. Bake at 350 degrees in preheated oven for 35 to 40 minutes.

Howard B. Mitchell
Former NSO Music Director
1949-1969

Italian Cheese Pie

SERVES 6 TO 8

CRUST
10-12 graham crackers

4 tablespoons butter, softened

PIE
8 ounces ricotta cheese

8 ounces cream cheese

2 tablespoons sour cream

2 eggs

¾ cup sugar

2 tablespoons lemon juice

1 teaspoon vanilla

TOPPING
½ pint sour cream

1 tablespoon lemon juice

2 tablespoons sugar

1 teaspoon vanilla

Cinnamon sugar

Crush graham crackers and mix with butter. Use mixture to line a 10-inch pie plate.

Mix ricotta and cream cheeses. Add eggs, sugar, sour cream, vanilla and lemon juice. Mix well; pour into crust and bake in a 375 degree oven for 20 minutes.

While pie is baking, make topping. Mix sour cream, sugar, vanilla and lemon juice.

Remove pie from oven and set oven at 450 degrees. Pour topping over pie and sprinkle with cinnamon sugar. After oven reaches 450 degrees, return pie to oven for another 4 minutes. Cool and refrigerate.

David Bragunier
Former NSO Principal Tuba

Grandmother's Lemon Pie

SERVES 12

CRUST
½ cup (1 stick) butter

3-ounce package cream cheese

1 cup flour

FILLING
8 eggs, separated

Pinch of salt

Juice of 4 lemons

¾ cup sugar

Rind of 2 lemons

1 tablespoon flour

½ cup superfine sugar

½ teaspoon baking powder

Small lump of butter

PIE CRUST

Mix ingredients together; roll out to fit a 10-inch pie plate; line pan and bake in a 425 degree oven for about 12 to 15 minutes or until golden brown. If crust starts to burn around the edges, turn heat down to 375 to 350 degrees.

FILLING

Beat egg yolks until thick and light. Add salt, sugar, flour, juice, rind of lemons and small lump of butter. Place in top of a double boiler. Cook until very, very thick and mixture coats a spoon. Let it cool.

While mixture is cooling, beat egg whites until stiff but not dry; add superfine sugar and baking powder. Fold ½ of egg-white mixture into cooled, lemon filling; put filling into crust. Place balance of egg-white mixture on top of pie; cover all crust. Bake in a hot (450 degree) oven until golden brown.

Mrs. Theodore L. Kaye

Hazelnut Fruit Tart

SERVES 8

2 cups flour

2 tablespoons sugar

¼ teaspoon salt

4 ounces unsalted butter

1 large egg

1 tablespoon cold water

4 ounces ground, toasted hazelnuts

1 tablespoon egg white

2 tablespoons sugar

12 ounces cream cheese

⅔ cup sugar

1 teaspoon vanilla

Seasonal fruits, as needed

¾ cup apple jelly, melted

¼ cup ground, toasted hazelnuts

Preheat oven to 400 degrees. Combine flour, 2 tablespoons sugar and salt. Crumble butter into flour mixture. Stir in egg and water. Blend in 4 ounces hazelnuts and refrigerate one hour.

Roll out dough and pat into 14-inch tart pan. Brush with egg white and sprinkle with 2 tablespoons sugar. Bake at 400 degrees for 20 minutes. Let cool; flip shell out of pan.

For filling, beat cream cheese, ⅔ cup sugar and vanilla until smooth and no lumps remain. Place filling on fruit tart shell and spread to edges. Place fruit in concentric circles on top of cream cheese. Brush melted apple jelly over fruits as glaze. Cover circle edge of tart with ¼ cup hazelnuts.

Refrigerate for at least 30 minutes before serving.

The Pleasant Pheasant Restaurant

Plum Tart with Almond Cream Base

SERVES 8

1½ cups flour

¼ teaspoon baking powder

½ cup butter, frozen, if using food processor

1 egg

⅓ cup sugar

Dash salt

1½-2 pounds Italian prunes (plums)

¼ cup cinnamon-sugar

Peel of orange or lemon, grated, optional

ALMOND CREAM
¾ cup blanched almonds, pulverized

⅓ cup sugar

1 egg

2 tablespoons butter

¼ teaspoon almond extract

Sift flour and baking powder together; blend in ½ cup butter. Beat egg separately; then add ⅓ cup sugar and salt; beat together. Add this to flour and make dough. Dough may be refrigerated for later use or it can be spread immediately into a 10-inch false-bottom tart pan.

Blend almond cream ingredients in food processor. Spread evenly into unbaked tart shell. Place plums circularly over almond cream and then sprinkle top with about ¼ cup cinnamon sugar. You may also want to add lemon peel.

Bake tart at 400 degrees for 15 minutes; lower temperature to 350 degrees and bake 40 minutes longer. Cool. When pastry shrinks from sides of pan, lift out. Serve at room temperature; refrigerate otherwise.

Tart may be made without almond base. If so, add ½ cup cinnamon sugar on top to offset tartness of plums. May be served with sweetened whipped cream.

Lonie Landfield

Plum Tart

SERVES 8

CRUST

1¼ cups flour

¼ teaspoon salt

½ cup (1 stick) cold unsalted butter, cut into pieces

2 tablespoons sour cream

FILLING

¼ cup flour

¼ teaspoon salt

3 large egg yolks

⅓ cup sour cream

1 cup sugar

15 Italian plums, pitted, sliced in half, sprinkled with a tablespoon or two of sugar and cinnamon

Preheat oven to 375 degrees. Using the metal blade of the food processor, process the flour, salt and butter until crumbly. Add the sour cream and let the machine run until the dough begins to form a smooth ball. Gather the dough into a flat disk.

On a floured surface roll out dough and place it in a 9-inch tart pan with a removable bottom. With your fingers press out dough to cover the bottom and sides evenly. Bake the crust in the center of the preheated oven for 20 minutes, or until lightly browned. Let cool on a wire rack for 15 minutes. Reduce oven temperature to 350 degrees.

Using the metal blade, process the egg yolks, sour cream, sugar, flour and salt for 5 seconds. Scrape down the sides of processor bowl. Let machine run 10 seconds. Pour half of the custard over the baked crust. Arrange the plums on top in circles. Pour remaining custard evenly over plums.

Bake the tart 40 to 50 minutes, or until the custard is set and the top lightly browned. Allow to cool 10 minutes before removing sides of pan. Serve at room temperature. Refrigerate if you do not plan to eat it within a few hours.

Susan Porter
NSO Board Member

Apfelküchen (Apple Tart)

Serves 8

PASTRY DOUGH

1½ cups all-purpose flour

Dash of salt

¾ cup (1½ sticks) butter

3 tablespoons cold water

LAYER

2 pounds apples

3 tablespoons apricot marmalade

3 tablespoons Calvados

Roasted almonds for decoration

Stir together flour and salt; cut in butter until pieces are size of small peas. Sprinkle with water and mix together rapidly. Dough should be pliable (neither dry nor sticky). Wrap in plastic and refrigerate for 12 hours.

Roll chilled dough thinly, about ⅟₁₆ inch, into rectangle and place on a cookie sheet.

Core and peel apples; cut into thin, long slices and cover dough. Place in preheated oven and bake for 20 minutes at 450 degrees. Lower temperature to 400 degrees and bake for 10 to 15 minutes.

While Apfelküchen is baking, heat apricot marmalade with Calvados. Strain sauce and glaze warm cake and decorate with roasted almonds. Serve warm.

Embassy of Austria

Pêches au Vin de Bordeaux

SERVES 4 TO 6

6 large, ripe peaches

4 cup red Bordeaux

1 pound granulated sugar

4 tablespoons cognac

Boil enough water to cover peaches. Drop peaches in boiling water for 1 minute. Drain, cool and peel.

Boil red Bordeaux and sugar for 5 minutes in a deep saucepan. Drop peaches in this red wine syrup. Simmer for 5 minutes or until tender. Remove fruits and place them in a jar. Heat syrup to 230 degrees and then cool thoroughly. To each cup of syrup add 1 tablespoon cognac. Fill jar to top until fruits are well covered.

Place jar in refrigerator. Serve peaches chilled and in syrup or garnished with whipped cream or scoops of vanilla ice cream.

Peaches will taste much better if they macerate in their syrup for about a week in the refrigerator.

Embassy of France

Saffron Broiled Pineapple

SERVES 6

1 pineapple

1 cup white wine

1 cup sugar

1 vanilla bean, split and seeds scraped

1 pinch saffron thread

Cut skin off pineapple; slice pineapple and core into ½ to ¾ inch slices. Each slice should have a hole near the center.

Bring white wine to boil. Add sugar, vanilla bean and saffron. Marinate the pineapple in the saffron wine liquid, preferably overnight.

Place marinade with pineapple in pan and reduce to sauce consistency.

Remove pineapple and sprinkle with sugar (in the raw) and place under broiler until slightly brown.

Serve with vanilla frozen yogurt, sorbet or ice cream.

Chef Frederic Przyborowski
Rock Creek Restaurant

Chocolate Cherry Clafoutis

SERVES 12

1 pint milk

1 pint heavy cream

½ cup sugar

10 egg yolks

1 pound bitter chocolate, chopped

1 10-ounce jar sweet cherries (maraschino cherries are not recommended)

Bring milk, heavy cream and ¼ cup sugar to a boil. In a bowl whisk together the remaining sugar and egg yolks. After liquid comes to a boil, add slowly into egg yolk mixture while whisking constantly. Then pour mixture back into the pot.

While stirring constantly over medium heat, cook until it coats the back of the spoon well. Do not allow mixture to boil or simmer. When proper consistency is reached, pour over chopped chocolate. Mix until chocolate is fully blended. Pour into any container selected. Then add strained cherries. Chill and serve.

Using brandied cherries is a great option for more flavor. Other fruit substitutes that may be used are peaches, pears or plums.

Jérôme Girardot
The Ritz-Carlton

Strawberries with Balsamic Vinegar

SERVES 4

1½ pints of strawberries

4 tablespoons balsamic vinegar

2 tablespoons sugar

Wash all of the strawberries thoroughly. In a large bowl, cut each strawberry in 4 to 6 pieces, depending on size. Add the balsamic vinegar and sugar. Let marinate for 5 minutes. Stir and mix until sugar is dissolved in vinegar and strawberries are completely coated in mixture.

Chef Fabrizio Aielli
Teatro Goldoni Restaurant

PUDDINGS, MOUSSES & SOUFFLÉS

Chestnut Mousse

SERVES 6 TO 8

15½-ounce can unsweetened chestnut purée

2 cups milk

8 tablespoons sugar

1 envelope unflavored gelatin, softened

1 teaspoon vanilla

6 egg yolks

3 tablespoons Grand Marnier

1 cup heavy cream

2 cups crème anglais

In blender blend chestnut purée with milk. Add sugar. Put mixture in pot. Beat with a wire whisk until smooth. Add gelatin, bring to a boil and stir in vanilla.

Beat egg yolks in a mixing bowl and beat in a little of hot sauce. Take pan off stove and add egg yolk mixture to hot sauce, stirring rapidly. Return pan to low heat and stir until mixture thickens slightly. Do not boil. Stir in liqueur.

Strain mixture through a sieve into mixing bowl and let cool but not set. Whip cream and fold into mousse mixture. Pour into lightly oiled 1½-quart mold and refrigerate several hours or overnight. Serve with crème anglais, found in most cookbooks, or whipped cream on the side.

Michael Phillips
Former NSO FANS Member

Crema Española (Spanish Cream Egg Custard)

SERVES 4

1 quart plus ¼ cup fresh whole milk

½ cup sugar

2 cinnamon sticks

3-inch vanilla bean, cut lengthwise

4-6 egg yolks

½ teaspoon lemon rind

3 heaping tablespoons cornstarch

½ teaspoon cinnamon

In a heavy 2-quart saucepan heat 1 quart milk, sugar, cinnamon sticks, vanilla bean, egg yolks and lemon rind.

In a small bowl mix starch and ¼ cup milk until smooth and free of lumps. Pour starch mixture very slowly into heating milk while stirring. Continue to stir over medium-high heat until custard begins to thicken. Reduce heat and continue stirring (until about consistency of condensed milk).

Remove from heat. Let stand uncovered for about ½ hour before placing in refrigerator to chill (3 hours). Sprinkle powdered cinnamon over custard. Serve with pirouettes or vanilla wafers.

Clemencia Sanchez

Angela Pia

SERVES 6 TO 8

1 tablespoon unflavored gelatin

¼ cup cold water

3 eggs, separated

½ cup superfine sugar

½ pint heavy whipping cream

1 ounce brandy

1 ounce rum

1 tablespoon vanilla

Toasted slivered almonds for garnish

Shaved semi-sweet chocolate for garnish

Place the gelatin and cold water in a heat-proof cup to dissolve. Place the cup into a small pan of hot water until the gelatin has melted. Set aside to cool for 5 to 10 minutes. Beat the egg whites until stiff and set aside. Beat the egg yolks, add the sugar gradually until thick and pale yellow in color.

Whip the cream until stiff and add the brandy, rum and vanilla. Stir the melted gelatin into the yolk mixture and gently fold in the whites and whipped cream. Pour into 8 sherbet glasses and cover with plastic wrap. Garnish before serving.

Susan Porter
NSO Board Member

Crème Brûlée

SERVES 6 TO 8

4 cups heavy cream

8 egg yolks

¼ cup plus 1 tablespoon sugar

2 teaspoons vanilla extract

Light brown sugar for topping, approximately ¾ cup

Adjust rack to the center of the oven and preheat to 325 degrees. Over low heat in a heavy saucepan, scald the cream (uncovered), until a thin wrinkled skin appears on top or until you see tiny bubbles around the edges.

In a large bowl, stir the egg yolks with a wire whisk just to mix. Add sugar to the scalded cream and stir to dissolve. Gradually, just a spoonful at a time and later in a steady, slow stream, stir the hot cream into the yolks. Do not beat; this mixture should not be foamy. Mix in the vanilla.

The custard should be baked in a shallow, ovenproof casserole with a 6 cup capacity or in individual ramekins. Pie plates also work well.

Fill the casserole or individual ramekins with the cream. Set into a larger baking dish in order to make a bain-marie. Now add hot water to the water bath so it comes half-way up the sides of the custard dish.

Bake for 30 minutes. If your casserole dish is deep, it may need a longer baking time. It is ready when a sharp knife inserted into the center comes out clean. Remove from the bain-marie onto a rack. When cool, refrigerate 8 hours or overnight.

Use approximately ¾ cup brown sugar for the topping. Push the sugar through a strainer to make an even layer ¼ of an inch thick. Broil only a few minutes until the sugar is melted. Do not take your eyes off of this for an instant. Leave oven door ajar so you can watch it. Cool to room temperature and then refrigerate 4 to 8 hours.

Crème Brûlée should be served very cold. If it is left in the refrigerator more than 6 to 8 hours, the sugars begin to melt. Although it will not be as crisp, it is still delicious and some people prefer it this way.

Susan Porter
NSO Board Member

Mousseline au Chocolat

SERVES 6 TO 8

6 ounces semi-sweet baking chocolate (1 cup chocolate chips)

4 tablespoons strong coffee

4 egg yolks

¾ cup superfine sugar

¼ cup orange liqueur, rum, Benedictine or strong coffee

6 ounces softened unsalted butter

4 egg whites

Pinch of salt

2 tablespoons finely granulated sugar

Stir chocolate and coffee in a small saucepan over hot water. When partially melted, set chocolate aside in its pan of water, stirring occasionally.

Beat egg yolks and sugar until they are thick, pale, and form a ribbon. Beat in liqueur or coffee. Set bowl over pan of simmering water and beat until foamy and almost too hot for your finger. Set bowl over cold water and continue beating until mixture is cool and again forms ribbons. It should be consistency of mayonnaise.

Stir chocolate again until perfectly smooth. Gradually beat in softened butter. Beat chocolate and butter into egg yolk mixture. Beat egg whites and salt until soft peaks form; sprinkle on sugar and beat until stiff peaks form. Stir one quarter of beaten egg whites into chocolate mixture; delicately fold in rest of egg whites.

Turn into a bowl or individual serving cups. Chill several hours or overnight.

Mrs. David R. Williams, Jr.

White Chocolate Mousse

SERVES 12 TO 16

This is a recipe for the experienced cook!

3 ounces (⅓ cup) skinned, toasted hazelnuts

⅓ cup skinned, toasted almonds

½ cup sugar

5 egg whites

Pinch of salt

3 ounces (⅓ cup) sugar

1 pound white chocolate

1 quart heavy cream

1 drop vanilla

To make praline, crush coarsely hazelnuts and almonds. Caramelize ⅓ cup sugar and combine with nuts. Pour onto oiled marble slab. Wait one hour and then crush praline coarsely.

Grate chocolate.

Whip egg whites and pinch of salt until firm. Immediately add second ⅓ cup sugar (that has been cooked to hard crack stage) to egg whites. Keep beating (don't worry if it deflates). Add chocolate and put bowl over boiling water to melt chocolate.

Whip cream with vanilla until thick. Pour egg white mixture over cream and fold with rubber spatula. When blended, add crushed praline. Pour into serving bowl and refrigerate 6 hours before serving.

Chef Yannick Cam
Le Pavillon Restaurant

Easy Lemon Mousse

SERVES 4 TO 6

5 eggs

2 lemons

1 teaspoon lemon rind, grated

½ cup sugar

1 cup whipping cream

Separate eggs; beat egg yolks with sugar until fluffy. Add juice of 2 lemons and 1 teaspoon grated rind to yolks. Heat over hot water (double boiler). Stir until thick. Cool.

Beat egg whites. Beat whipped cream separately. Fold egg mixture into whipped cream. Fold egg whites into all of above. Chill 4 hours.

Kathy Butler Phelan

Maple Syrup Mousse

SERVES 6 TO 8

♪

This mousse is not as sweet as you may think, and it tastes like coffee mousse!

1 envelope plus 2 teaspoons unflavored gelatin

½ cup water

1 cup pure maple syrup

4 egg yolks

½ cup dark brown sugar

4 egg whites

2 cups chilled heavy cream (60% butterfat, optional)

OPTIONAL
¼ cup Kahlua and ¼ cup water for ½ cup water

Sprinkle gelatin into ½ cup of cold water. Let it soften for about 5 minutes. Set cup in a shallow pan of simmering water and stir until gelatin has dissolved and is clear. Combine with maple syrup. In a large mixing bowl, beat egg yolks with a whisk or beater for 2 or 3 minutes until thick and lemon yellow.

Beat into yolks maple syrup mixture and pour into a small saucepan. Cook over moderate heat, stirring constantly, until mixture thickens enough to coat spoon heavily. Do not let it boil or eggs will curdle. Remove from heat, stir in brown sugar and mix thoroughly. Transfer to a large bowl and cool to room temperature.

Meanwhile, beat egg whites until they form firm peaks. In another bowl, whip chilled cream until it holds its shape softly. With a rubber spatula, fold cream gently but thoroughly into maple syrup mixture; then fold in egg whites, folding until streaks of white no longer show.

Rinse a 1½-quart mold, preferable a charlotte mold, in cold water. Shake out excess water and pour in mousse mixture. Chill in refrigerator for at least 4 hours, or until firm.

To unmold, run a knife around inside edge of mold, dip bottom briefly in hot water and wipe it dry. Place a chilled platter on top of mold, invert and rap it on the table. Chill until ready to serve. Decorate with whipped cream and chocolate curls, if desired.

Barry E. Huber
Former NSO FANS Member

Mousse de Pruneau à l'Armagnac

MAKES 2 QUARTS OF ICE CREAM

1 pound dried prunes, preferably sour

2 cups milk

1 vanilla bean split down middle or 1 teaspoon vanilla extract

12 egg yolks

⅓ cup granulated sugar

⅔ cup light corn syrup

2 cups heavy cream

Armagnac

Marinate prunes in Armagnac to cover for at least 2 weeks, adding more Armagnac as required.

Prepare ice cream one day in advance of serving. In a small saucepan, heat milk with vanilla bean; remove from heat. Lift out vanilla bean; scrape seeds into milk, discard shell and set vanilla-flavored hot milk aside, covered.

In heavy-bottomed, 3-quart saucepan, whisk together egg yolks, sugar and a pinch of salt until pale yellow and creamy. Gradually add hot milk in a steady steam, whisking constantly. Add corn syrup; slowly heat, stirring with a wooden spoon, until mixture thickens sufficiently, registering about 175 degrees. Do not allow to boil. Remove from heat; strain through fine sieve into chilled mixing bowl to stop cooking. Cool. Stir in heavy cream. Cover with plastic wrap and chill about 2 hours.

Pour mixture into container of an electric or hand-operated ice cream churner and freeze until mush, operating machine according to manufacturer's directions.

Remove prunes from Armagnac and pit them; reserve Armagnac. In work bowl of a food processor fitted with the metal blade, process prunes for 10 seconds, or until well chopped. When ice cream is half frozen, add chopped prunes and ¼ cup of Armagnac. (Use remaining Armagnac as a syrup for ice cream.)

Pack ice cream into a 2-quart ice cream mold and freeze until hard, preferably overnight.

One-half hour before serving, transfer ice cream to refrigerator compartment to soften slightly. Invert onto a serving plate. To help loosen ice cream, soak a kitchen cloth in hot water, wring out and wrap around mold. If necessary, tap mold lightly with your fingers and shake it to loosen. If surface needs a little patching up, smooth it with a spatula dipped in hot water. Return ice cream to freezer for 5 minutes to firm up. Serve each portion with a drizzle of remaining Armagnac.

Albert J. Beveridge, III
Former NSO Board Member

Soufflé – Orange and Chocolate

SERVES 4

PASTRY CREAM
2 cups milk

3 eggs

1 egg yolk

½ cup sugar

¾ cup flour

SOUFFLÉ
2 cups pastry cream

3 egg yolks

5 egg whites

FOR CHOCOLATE SOUFFLÉ
VANILLA SAUCE
1 cup milk

1 vanilla bean

4 egg yolks

¼ cup sugar

CHOCOLATE
5 tablespoons melted chocolate

FOR ORANGE SOUFFLÉ
2 tablespoons candied orange rind

3 tablespoons Cointreau

Orange sections

Apricot liqueur

Cognac

Confectioners sugar

PASTRY CREAM
Bring milk to boil. Mix eggs and sugar until smooth. Add flour and mix until smooth. Pour boiling milk into mixture. While mixing, put back on stove and boil again, stirring constantly.

SOUFFLÉ
Add egg yolk to pastry cream and heat. Whip egg whites until stiff and add 2 tablespoons sugar. For orange soufflé add orange rind and Cointreau to pastry cream. For chocolate soufflé add melted chocolate to pastry cream. Add one quarter of egg white and mix well. Fold in rest of egg whites. Butter and coat your soufflé dish with sugar. Pour soufflé into dish (for orange, add fresh orange sections). Fill to top and smooth with a spatula. Bake in a 375 degree oven for 20 minutes.

FOR CHOCOLATE SOUFFLÉ
Boil milk with vanilla bean. Mix egg yolks and sugar. Pour boiling milk over mixture. Mix well, put back on stove and cook until it thickens without boiling. Add 2 tablespoons cognac.

FOR ORANGE SOUFFLÉ
Sprinkle with confectioners sugar. For decoration place a few orange sections and candied orange rinds around. Flambé with Cointreau and serve.

For apricot sauce, whip cream mixed with apricot glaze and apricot liqueur.

Chef Jean-Pierre Goyenvalle
Le Lion d'Or Restaurant

Prepare-Ahead Chocolate Soufflé

Serves 8

5 egg yolks

¾ cup sugar

4 drops vanilla

1 cup unbleached flour

2 cups milk

2 ounces unsweetened chocolate, melted

8 egg whites

Confectioners sugar

½ pint heavy cream, whipped

In a bowl beat yolks with ½ cup sugar and vanilla until light and fluffy. Gradually beat in flour until a paste is formed.

Meanwhile, bring milk to boil. Add egg mixture all at once and bring again to boil, beating vigorously with wire whisk until paste is smooth. Continue stirring with wooden spoon until mixture is thick, like a pastry cream. Add melted chocolate and stir until blended. Cool.

Beat egg whites until soft peaks form; gradually beat in remaining ¼ cup sugar until stiff peaks form. Fold egg whites into batter. Cover bowl lightly and allow to sit at room temperature for up to 4 hours before serving.

To serve, spoon into 8 greased, individual, 2-inch soufflé dishes and bake at 350 degrees for 20 minutes. Dust with confectioners sugar and serve with whipped cream on the side.

Marian Burros
Former Food Journalist, The New York Times

Orange Marmalade Soufflé

SERVES 4 TO 5

4 egg whites

4 tablespoons sugar

4 tablespoons orange marmalade

4 egg yolks

½ cup confectioners sugar

1 jigger rum (2 ounces)

1 cup whipped cream

Beat egg whites until stiff. Add sugar. Fold marmalade into mixture. Generously butter top of a 2-quart double boiler and sprinkle with sugar. Put mixture in pan when water is boiling rapidly. Do not let water touch bottom of pan or evaporate completely. Put lid on pan. Simmer gently 1 hour. Do not remove lid. Turn onto a platter when done.

SAUCE

Beat yolks well. Add sugar, rum and whipped cream. Pour a little sauce on top of unmolded soufflé. Serve rest in a sauce bowl. Sauce can be prepared a few hours before and refrigerated.

Juliet P. Hart
Former NSO FANS Member

Cold Lemon Soufflé

SERVES 6

6 eggs, separated

1½ cups sugar

3 lemons, finely grated (squeeze and reserve juice)

1 envelope unflavored gelatin

1 pint heavy cream, whipped

2 packages lady fingers

1 package frozen raspberries, puréed

1 cup orange juice

FILLING

Mix egg yolks and sugar in top of double boiler until well blended; cool for 15 minutes. Add rind of lemon. In a saucepan, mix reserved juice and gelatin and cook over low heat until dissolved. Beat the egg whites. Beat the cream until thick. Add gelatin to sugar and egg mixture. Fold in the egg whites and cream.

Line a 9-inch springform pan or cake mold with the ladyfingers. Sprinkle the ladyfingers with orange juice. Add layer of filling. Continue repeating process.

Put in freezer for about 3 hours. Unmold and serve with rasberry purée.

Frances Sniffen
NSO Women's Committee Member

INDEX

INDEX

INDEX

INDEX

THE NATIONAL SYMPHONY ORCHESTRA COOKBOOK

ORDER FORM

Please send me_____copies of the cookbook at $19.95 each, plus shipping and handling stated below:
(1 copy - $5.00; 2 -$6.00; 3-5 - $8.00; free for over five copies all going to the same address)

Quantity	Item	Price	Shipping	Total Payment
	NSO Cookbook	$19.95		

NAME   PHONE

ADDRESS

CITY   STATE   ZIP CODE

Mail with check payable to The Kennedy Center Gift Shop to: Kennedy Center • **Attention:** Gift Shop PO Box 101510, Arlington, VA 22210. To order using a credit card, visit: www.kennedy-center.org/giftshop or call (202) 416-8343.

THE NATIONAL SYMPHONY ORCHESTRA COOKBOOK

ORDER FORM

Please send me_____copies of the cookbook at $19.95 each, plus shipping and handling stated below:
(1 copy - $5.00; 2 -$6.00; 3-5 - $8.00; free for over five copies all going to the same address)

Quantity	Item	Price	Shipping	Total Payment
	NSO Cookbook	$19.95		

NAME   PHONE

ADDRESS

CITY   STATE   ZIP CODE

Mail with check payable to The Kennedy Center Gift Shop to: Kennedy Center • **Attention:** Gift Shop PO Box 101510, Arlington, VA 22210. To order using a credit card, visit: www.kennedy-center.org/giftshop or call (202) 416-8343.

THE NATIONAL SYMPHONY ORCHESTRA COOKBOOK

ORDER FORM

Please send me_____copies of the cookbook at $19.95 each, plus shipping and handling stated below:
(1 copy - $5.00; 2 -$6.00; 3-5 - $8.00; free for over five copies all going to the same address)

Quantity	Item	Price	Shipping	Total Payment
	NSO Cookbook	$19.95		

NAME   PHONE

ADDRESS

CITY   STATE   ZIP CODE

Mail with check payable to The Kennedy Center Gift Shop to: Kennedy Center • **Attention:** Gift Shop PO Box 101510, Arlington, VA 22210. To order using a credit card, visit: www.kennedy-center.org/giftshop or call (202) 416-8343.